IN THE BLINK OF AN EYE

IN THE BLINK OF AN EYE

AN AUTOBIOGRAPHY
MAHMOUD ABDUL·RAUF
WITH NICK CHILES

KAEPERNICK
PUBLISHING

WWW.KAEPERNICKPUBLISHING.COM
PRINTED IN THE UNITED STATES OF AMERICA

IN THE BLINK OF AN EYE
ISBN: 978-1595911209

LIBRARY OF CONGRESS CATALOGUING-IN-PUBLICATION
DATA IS AVAILABLE FOR THIS TITLE.

10 9 8 7 6 5 4 3 2 1

COVER ART BY A. DANIEL DICKSON II
COVER IMAGE FROM SCOTT OLSON / REUTERS PICTURES
BOOK PRODUCED BY MELCHER MEDIA
DISTRIBUTED BY TWO RIVERS DISTRIBUTION

To the woman who will always have my heart, my mom,
Ms. Jacqueline Jackson.

To my children—Ali Abdul-Rauf, Alim Abdul-Rauf,
Ammar Abdul-Rauf, Safiyyah Abdul-Rauf, Amir Abdul-Rauf,
and the two we lost and with whom we are waiting to be
reunited—who have been a major source of inspiration,
even before they were conceived.

FOREWORD

I've been waiting for this book for a long time—and now it is here. Years ago, when basketball meant everything to me, I remember Chris Jackson, and I'm fairly certain I remember when: NBC Saturday afternoon. LSU was playing whoever they were playing, and the broadcasters, Dick Enberg and Al McGuire, were raving about no. 35, Chris Jackson.

I remember seeing him: clear and present but unassuming on the court—none of that performative mean-mugging for the cameras, the artificial anger-branding so common and expected with athletes, Black athletes in particular. Jackson seemed almost out of place—and he was, because when he got the ball, he was so explosive, moving at a different speed from the other nine guys on the court. He was playing a different game, in complete control of the action, and his place in the action. Most players have a favorite place to operate—Jordan at the elbow, Kareem on the right block, and years later, LeBron from up top—but every spot on the court belonged to Jackson. The crossover, the hesitation to clear space to find his shot, the confidence to shoot from range, and naturally, the perfect mechanics on release. I'd never seen anything like it. He was mesmerizing.

When he changed his name to Mahmoud Abdul-Rauf and joined the NBA, he was no less fascinating—still able to do in the NBA what he'd done in college. He crushed Utah so bad one night and made cheap-shotting John Stockton increase his cheap-shot quotient. It did no good. Mahmoud finished with 51.

Basketball became less important—I wasn't a kid anymore, but I still paid attention to Mahmoud. More specifically, I paid attention to how differently Mahmoud was perceived by a simple name change. There were the people who simply refused to call him by his

Muslim name, a curious insult considering it was nearly a quarter century after Kareem and almost 30 years since Muhammad Ali had to fight for their names to be recognized. These battles, supposedly, had already been fought—and won.

Mahmoud was there—until he wasn't, and in his absence, I recalled the casual explanations for his disappearance from the league. He was difficult. He couldn't play anymore. He was the author of his own demise. The volume of this voice and the power of the NBA left this a satisfactory explanation for anyone whose allegiance was simply to being entertained watching Black men put a ball through a hoop. For the rest of us, who care about people, authenticity, and their life's journeys, the truth wasn't that narrative. Mahmoud Abdul-Rauf's career was altered because he advocated for Black people, for his beliefs, and for his values. We wanted to know where he was. We wanted to hear from him.

Into a new century, the 1990s look very different now. They carry the introspection they lacked in real time, and as is often the case with people of substance, people of principle, they grow over the years. The questions surrounding Mahmoud are no longer only about him, but about the world around him. Where was his support, the super-big names who dominated the game? Why was Mahmoud left isolated? Who came to his defense, and where was everyone else? Were his fellow NBA players all so busy with the cosplay of wearing $3,000 suits, pretending to look like board members in a room to which they've never been invited, while abandoning one of their own?

Unlike today, Mahmoud received no celebrity safety net, where principled people discarded by their leagues are rescued— transferred into another high-profile second act. Mahmoud, like Craig Hodges before him, endured the full brunt of a hostile culture without the benefit of public support, or the comfort of knowing that behind the scenes his more powerful peers had his back.

It is with that spirit in mind that I have long welcomed the arrival of this book. Mahmoud Abdul-Rauf in his own words is long overdue, but while we absorb this new decade where the athlete voice has again been heard, beginning with the killing of Trayvon Martin, through Ferguson, and the deaths of Eric Garner, Sandra Bland, Tamir Rice, Freddie Gray, and, unnecessarily, so many others, it is important to remember that special individuals have been standing up for years—only no one was listening.

Now people are, and the years after Ahmaud Arbery, Breonna Taylor, and George Floyd will undoubtedly focus on reconnecting the lineage we know: Jackie Robinson to Muhammad Ali to Tommie Smith and John Carlos in the civil rights movement to LeBron and Kaepernick today. The history will be told incorrectly, as if protest has occurred in a straight, unbreakable, supported, and respected line. It hasn't.

The iconic beginning of the athlete as a political and social force, and its current revival, will take up most of the space because it is the easiest material to Google—but don't forget those barren years in between, and the solitary athletes who stood fighting by themselves, when America and its richer, more visible peers couldn't be bothered because the money was too big and the pressure to conform was too great. In other words, don't forget Mahmoud. I certainly haven't. Now that he is telling his story, his way, on his terms, you won't, either.

HOWARD BRYANT
AMHERST, MASSACHUSETTS
FEBRUARY II, 2022

The morning shootaround was when I first noticed the crowd of reporters clustered on the sidelines, watching closely as my teammates and I went through our warm-up routine on the court. The shootaround was usually a casual affair: a light workout, maybe we'd run through a few plays we would use in the game that night. We were playing the Orlando Magic, which meant Shaq was in town. Shaquille O'Neal usually brought a larger than normal contingent of media wherever he went, but it was unusual to see a knot of reporters this size at McNichols Sports Arena in Denver on a Tuesday morning, even if it was for the Shaq show.

An air of anticipation hovered over the reporters, like they were sprinters waiting for the starting gun. When Coach Bernie Bickerstaff ended the shootaround, the gun had been sounded.

The reporters all scurried straight toward me. *Wait, they're here for me? What in the world for?*

It didn't take long to find out.

As soon as I sat down, they gathered around and started flinging questions at me.

"So, what do you think about the flag?"

Ahh, the flag. Yes, of course. A few days earlier, Todd Eley, the assistant general manager of the Nuggets, had approached me and said one of the local radio reporters wanted to talk to me. The reporter had noticed I wasn't standing during the national anthem; he wanted to know why.

"Would you be interested in speaking to him about it?" Eley asked.

"I don't have a problem talking to anybody about it," I said.

The interview wasn't that long. I told him why I didn't stand for the flag — the same thing I told the reporters that morning after the shootaround. When his story came out, the news reverberated across the country, and I had become a pawn in America's culture wars.

"Look, the flag is a symbol of tyranny and oppression," I told the group. "Am I saying everything in America's bad? No. There's good that exists. But as a Muslim, wherever bad is, even if it's in Saudi Arabia, we don't stand for it. We can't be for God and oppression at the same time. There's a verse in the Quran which says Allah didn't create the human being with two hearts. He only gave us one. So, you can't worship Satan and God at the same time. You know, it's a contradiction. You got to make a choice. You can't be neutral."

When I was done, I was satisfied that I had spoken my mind in an honest way, with a statement that was balanced but, most important, accurate. If any logical person was asked, "Is everything in America bad?" the answer of course would be "No." There is good in America as well as bad. But if your country prides itself on the language of justice — like American politicians and pundits say they do — then how can you not acknowledge the historical and present-day injustices some people in this country face so often? Allah says we must speak out against injustice, even if it's against yourself, your children, your family. Enjoining good and forbidding evil is one of the most serious obligations Allah decrees. That means as a nation, if you are truly committed to being virtuous, you must institutionalize justice and deconstruct the institutionalization of injustice.

Of course, white American politicians can speak all day long about America's wrongs. But, as I quickly learned, if a Black athlete making millions of dollars claims that America is corrupt, the sky will come crashing down on his head.

The reporters ran out of the gym like they had won the lottery. When they filed their reports, they did everything they could to maximize the drama. They focused on what I said about the flag representing tyranny and oppression, conveniently downplaying the rest of my statement, that there is good and bad in America.

When I left the arena after the shootaround, I still had no idea that I suddenly had a starring role in a brewing national controversy. After all, I was in my sixth season, and I had been opting not to stand for the anthem for more than a year. It was part of my intellectual awakening, as I learned of the hypocrisies and inequities embedded in every aspect of America's institutions. I was reading a great deal on a wide range of topics, ravenously trying to absorb as much as I could about so many issues about which I had been blind and ignorant. Three days before the controversy exploded, I had turned twenty seven. I felt reborn, like a sheath had been removed from my eyes.

I frequently shared the things I read with my teammates on the Nuggets, engaging them in deep discussions about the state of America and the world. They had long grown used to my politics and my refusal to stand for the flag. To them, it was old news. I felt the same. I was stunned that anybody could consider this earth shattering when I had been exhibiting my stance in full view of thousands of fans — and a full contingent of media — on a nightly basis. On top of that, I saw these same fans showing a regular and glaring disrespect for the flag by talking while the anthem was playing, walking around, booing, sitting down, or not being attentive at all.

After the shootaround, we customarily went back to our homes to eat and rest before the game. That's what I did that day, still unaware of what was happening to me. When I returned to the arena that night, Jim Gillen, the team trainer, approached me in the locker room.

"Hey, Bernie wants to see you," he said. I saw the concerned expression on his face. As I walked through the locker room, I saw what appeared to be grimaces on the faces of my teammates. *Uh-oh. Something is wrong.*

I walked into Bernie's office down the hall. He didn't waste any time. "We got a call from the NBA today," he said. "They want you to stand. And they said if you don't stand, they're going to suspend you." I shook my head. "Well, Bernie, they got to do what they got to do, because I'm not going to stand."

"There are a couple of people from the NBA office who want to talk to you," he said. "Do you mind getting on the phone?" Bernie had been my coach and/or general manager (he was serving in both roles that year) since I entered the league six years earlier. He knew me well. I suspect he had already told the NBA execs what my response was likely to be.

He called in to the NBA office. A couple of voices came on the speakerphone. I'm not sure who they were, but they said they were Jewish and tried to appeal to my religious faith by using the rules of Jewish Shabbat as an example. Though observant Jews follow the rules, exceptions are made. They were suggesting I could also make an exception. But their exception wasn't compatible with my faith.

After they made their case, I responded: "I appreciate you saying that, but there's only one problem . . ."

"What's that?"

"I'm not Jewish," I said. "That example doesn't apply to me." The speakerphone fell silent. They had nothing else.

"Okay," one of them said.

And that was that.

I looked at Bernie. "Y'all do what you have to do, man," I said. "Can I go get dressed now and get ready for the game?"

He said, "No, the suspension starts now."

"What? Now?" I said. I had never been suspended for anything and thought they would have to go through some type of
deliberation process. But clearly I was being naive. "Well, can I go
out and show support for the team by sitting in the stands?" I asked.
"No, they don't want you on the premises, on the property, or in the
stands." So, I walked out of his office. I went into the locker room
to get my stuff. A few of the guys were in there. "Hey, I'm out. Y'all
have a good one." They looked at me like I was crazy. "Yeah, I've
been suspended." I walked out and went straight to my car. There
would be no basketball for me that night.

Up to that point, with twenty-one games left in the season, I was having one of the best campaigns of my NBA career. I
was averaging 19.2 points per game, the most on the Nuggets—
almost 5 points more than Dale Ellis, the second-leading scorer. My
6.8 assists per game also led the team and was in the top twenty in
the NBA; Jalen Rose was second on the team at 6.2 assists per game.
I led the NBA in free throw shooting, at 93 percent, having missed
only 11 free throws the entire season. In fact, I believe I was the only
player in the league shooting above 90 percent from the line.

A few months earlier, in December, I had scored 51 points
against John Stockton, a future Hall of Fame point guard, as we beat
the Utah Jazz. In February, I scored 32 against Michael Jordan and
the Chicago Bulls, snapping their eighteen-game winning streak—
the game was called one of the biggest victories in the history of the
Nuggets franchise.

It wasn't my first run-in with the NBA front office. During the
previous season, my agent, Sharif Naseer, got a call from the NBA
because they were upset that I wasn't wearing my socks properly.
I would fold my socks down to be level with the tops of my shoes
because I didn't like my socks up too high. I have Tourette syndrome,

which sometimes drives me crazy if my clothes don't feel a certain way. Believe me, it's sometimes hard for me to understand, too. But when I folded down the socks, it covered up the NBA logo. They wanted to fine me a thousand dollars a sock if I continued to cover up the logo. Okay, I got it. The NBA is nothing if not a profit-making corporation. I agreed to leave the logo visible on my socks.

After they suspended me from the Orlando game, which cost me almost $32,000 of my $2.6 million salary, my agent called Rod Thorn, the NBA executive in charge of enforcing league rules. When he complained to Rod that I had been suspended for violating the league rule that players had to stand for the anthem, Rod responded that there was no such rule. This was the NBA rules chief, declaring that the league didn't have any rule on the books about standing for the anthem. Essentially the league had made it up to make an example out of me. In a league that is nearly 80 percent Black, I think NBA executives didn't want my refusal to stand to give other players any ideas about taking a similar action. In retrospect, I should have sued the mess out of the league, but at the time I just wanted to get back on the court with my principles intact.

The players union got involved in the controversy. After further discussion, I agreed that I would stand with the team during the anthem — but instead of placing my hand over my heart, I would hold out my hands in a gesture of prayer and pray for those who are dispossessed and those who are oppressed.

As I watched the news reports on my anthem boycott, I was upset that my character was being assassinated. I was being portrayed as some sort of troublemaker, a bad dude, rather than a man of faith who was taking a principled stand and exercising my freedom of speech rights. I thought the portraits of me were so off base, so far from the truth. The media was making little effort to find out who the real Mahmoud Abdul-Rauf was. I got a request from Larry

King Live to go on the air and explain my side of the story. As I pondered the request and my next step, I checked in with one of my mentors, Imam Muhammad al-Asi.

He told me the story of how the Prophet, while sitting with a companion, stood up out of respect when a Jewish funeral procession rolled by. His companion asked why he would stand for a nonbeliever. "Is it not a living being [soul]?" the Prophet responded. Al-Asi explained that the Prophet was not standing for their cause, he was standing because Allah gave a life and he took a life away. "You can stand and you can pray for those who are oppressed," al-Asi told me. "You can do this while still holding true to your principles and keeping the integrity of your faith strong."

When he said it like that, it made sense to me. He also said that going back to the team would bring more visibility to my cause. I knew that many would see it as me giving in to the NBA, caving, but those people wouldn't know the details of how it went down. I would tell anyone who asked that I still felt the same way about the flag and the system, but I was presented with another way to make my case.

Four years earlier, when I reverted—in Islam we don't use the term conversion because we believe to submit to Islam is to return to our natural state—I didn't know many Muslims. I didn't have any close friends who were Muslims. But I was open to meeting people and learning as much as I could. After my reversion became public and I changed my name, I would get approached by Muslims in every city the Nuggets traveled to for games. They would find out which hotel we were staying at and come up to me in the lobby, asking if they could speak with me. If I felt that they were genuine, I would engage them in a longer than normal conversation. If I had a strong connection with them, I might invite them up to my room if time permitted. That's how it would start. In some cases, I established long-term friendships this way.

We'd talk about everything: politics, world events, history, capitalism, and, of course, Islam and the Quran. I was learning a great deal from these conversations—more in this short amount of time than I ever had through all my years of schooling. Guys would mention books to me, and I'd go straight to the nearest bookstore to buy them. Sometimes they would give me books to read. The more I learned, the more I wanted to learn. The effects of slavery and poverty. The role of the World Bank and the International Monetary Fund. The purification of the heart. The power of propaganda. You name it, we discussed it.

One of my close friends in Denver was a Muslim named Bashir, who owned a bookstore, Salaam Books. I would go there from time to time, and I discovered many books on Israel and Zionism and an endless supply of fascinating books on many other topics. It all began to pierce my conscience. I was now getting the language to understand things that had bothered me when I was younger but didn't understand why. All the stuff I had always been taught about America being so exceptional, the best, the most righteous, the most ethical country in the world, I now began to take exception to. What bothered me was the idea of America's innocence. We Americans go around the world accusing other nations of evil, undemocratic acts, but when America does something even worse, we call it a mistake. As if it wasn't intentional.

In the context of all this education, as I absorbed this information, I began to see the act of standing and saluting the flag during the national anthem in a much different way. We are taught to stand for the flag, but most of us have never thought about what the flag means. It's just reflexive. Robotic. I looked at politicians and the political system and saw that in no way did the flag represent me, especially as a Black man in America. Maybe if I were white, I could see the privilege. Maybe I'd want to go out and be a part of that system and salute it because I could see how it benefits me. But how is it benefiting people who look like me? I said to myself, *I don't want to do this anymore. I'm not going to do this anymore.*

I knew that people would look at me and say, "Oh, you're making millions, the system is benefiting you." Yes, I may have found my way into a profession where I can personally profit, but I was no longer thinking in this individualistic way that American society encourages us to think. "Pull yourself up by your boostraps" — that moronic crap blinds us from seeing how the system is exploiting almost all of us to enrich the few. In Islam, society is more important than the individual. Muslims are encouraged to think about what will benefit the collective — though not at the expense of your individuality. Allah says, "Verily, Allah will not change the condition of a people until they change themselves." So, personal development is essential but only as it pertains to a higher purpose, which is the condition of people. It's similar to the Ubuntu concept "I am because we are."

After I made my decision to not stand during the anthem, I began to sit down and stretch while it was being played. Or I would turn the opposite way from my teammates and say prayers — just as long as I wasn't standing at attention. I had a variety of measures I used. After the controversy exploded, the media reported that I had been hiding in the locker room during the anthem, but that was a lie. I never did that — at least not intentionally. There may have been a couple of times when I went to the locker room to use the bathroom, but that was never some grand plan.

I had a couple of occasions when I was conflicted about what to do. One was when we played in Charlotte. In Charlotte, the teams line up in the middle of half-court for the anthem. After the controversy broke, reporters went back and found footage of me standing in the middle of the court, unsure of my next move. Finally, I walked off the court and went over to the bench because I couldn't take my uncertainty anymore.

During the media's intense focus on me and what position my body was in during the anthem, my relationship with my teammates was relatively unaffected. We were still joking and laughing together, engaging in deep conversations as well as lighthearted ones. We went about our business. Professional athletes are accustomed to being met with hostility on the road. When you go into another team's arena, the fans are going to boo at you and yell ridiculous things to try to rattle you. Every NBA player develops a thick armor to ward off all that stuff. You also get used to the media asking you questions after the game about all kinds of random or controversial things. If you don't want to answer, there is nothing requiring that you do.

When we played at home, I didn't hear any boos at McNichols when I came out onto the court. It felt to me that I still had the support of the Denver fans.

Knowing all that, I was surprised when I heard Coach Bickerstaff declare that the anthem controversy was proving to be a "distraction" to the team. Observing my teammates, I didn't think that was true at all. Dudes were doing what they always did, going to the movies, connecting with friends, and going out to dinner, while others perhaps were hitting the local strip clubs, hooking up with women, or drinking or smoking too much. But to team management, that stuff wasn't a distraction. My right hand failing to meet my left breast during the national anthem was. It didn't make sense to me.

One might think that since I was the team's leading scorer and one of its leading assist men, Nuggets management would be doing everything they could to keep me on the court. But that's not what happened.

One day, Coach Bickerstaff said he wanted to talk to me.

"Look, why don't you just forget this season," he said. "Just stay home. We'll end it now."

I was startled. We still had a few more weeks in the season. The team wasn't playing well—we were about ten games below .500—but I didn't see how things could get any better if I stayed home. Clearly, Bernie just didn't want me around.

I did as he suggested and stayed away from the team, spending most of my time at my house just outside Denver in Castle Rock, Colorado. I didn't know what was going to happen next, but I sensed that this was a pivotal moment for my career. I started to think about other athletes who had paid an enormous price, who'd had their careers disrupted in their prime for standing up for what they believed in. Men like Tommie Smith and John Carlos and Muhammad Ali. I wasn't by any means putting myself on their level, but I wondered if I was being set up for the same kind of punishment.

I was trying to stay away from the television, but I was aware of what people were saying about me. While a significant portion of the Black community seemed to have my back, many Muslims were telling interviewers that they were against what I was doing because it wasn't representative of Islam. Much of the condemnation came from Muslims who had migrated to the United States. While I was disappointed, it made sense to me. They were trying to assimilate, so they were disturbed to see this dude come along and draw undue attention to their religion. African Americans, on the other hand, had no fears about somebody deciding they should be sent back home— where could they send us? Where could they deport us to?

I saw interviews with Muslims who were claiming that there's nothing in the Quran that states we are to oppose nationalism. I couldn't believe what I was hearing. "Are you serious right now?" I said out loud to the TV. Quite the contrary, there are many verses instructing Muslims to oppose nationalism, tyranny, and oppression. Those are some of the fundamental lessons Muslims are taught— beliefs that drew me to Islam in the first place.

I told myself that I couldn't let such chatter unnerve me or cause me undue stress because it was something I could not change. I tried to use the time off from basketball to do more reading, but I was still working out, keeping in shape. I didn't do too much traveling at the time. In case the Nuggets suddenly decided that I should rejoin the team, I wanted to remain nearby. I didn't want to give them any excuses to claim that Mahmoud was unavailable and therefore had abandoned the team. I didn't trust them.

Though I tried to stay on an even keel as I listened to people who didn't know me try to assassinate my character and paint me as this bad dude, one day my body let me know that I wasn't being successful. While I was standing in the bathroom, a weird, unsettling feeling came over me. I started shaking and sweating profusely, like I had just played an entire game. The sweat was pouring down my face, into my eyes, and the room suddenly was unbearably hot. My stomach was tensing up, spasming. I could tell right away that something was wrong.

I was home alone. I struggled to my car and drove myself to the closest hospital, sweating through my clothes in the driver's seat, telling myself that I needed to remain calm. They put me in a room and connected me to an IV while they figured out what was wrong. One of the doctors came back into the room and announced that I had an ulcer. *What? An ulcer?* I thought I had been doing a good job of not letting this stuff get to me. Wrong.

They gave me some medicine to take and sent me back home. But a couple days later, it happened again. This time I felt even weirder. My gums started protruding, or at least it felt like they were, almost as if somebody was blowing them up like a balloon. My stomach was killing me even worse than before. At the hospital, they wanted to give me a bunch of drugs on top of the ones I was already taking. I was a bit skeptical, since the drugs hadn't worked the first time. I decided to call my older brother, David. After he got out of the military, David spent years studying natural medicine and had become an expert in homeopathy. As soon as the thought came to me, I realized I should have called him at the very start of the problem. I left the hospital again with more medicines, but this time I consulted with David. He told me to get some tea tree oil and rub it on my gums. Right away, the swelling of my gums receded, like David had flipped a switch. He told me to get a South American tree bark called *pau d'arco* and myrrh gum liquid. He said taking these would help clean my colon, which he said was where my problems were originating. My appetite quickly returned. "What did they give you in the hospital?" David asked. I told him the names of the medicines. He consulted a large pharmaceutical directory he had and told me some of the ingredients would do the job of helping to heal me. But then he pointed out several other ingredients in the same medicines: "Those are gonna cause problems."

I started getting angrier the more I heard. It was like they were playing Russian roulette with my health. "This is criminal— they're killing folks!" I said. "Why would I want to take this stuff?"

At that moment, I decided to seize control of my health. One way to do that was by carefully monitoring the things I put into my body. I was grateful David had been there for me to help me get through that medical emergency. I did not want the public to find out about my ulcer, so I didn't tell anybody, not even my agent or my teammates. But I knew it was a bad idea for me to try to hold everything in. Tourette had been teaching me that lesson for most of my life: you gotta let stuff go, otherwise it's going to bubble up and explode.

My decision making at this time was primarily about my conscience, my interpretation of how to live in a way that was consistent with my principles. I didn't think of myself as leading any kind of movement or trying to be some type of heroic figure. I knew there was a good chance that my stand would have an impact on people, perhaps make them think more deeply about what message they were saying when they stood for the national anthem. NBA legend Charles Barkley created quite a stir a few years earlier when he declared in a 1993 Nike commercial that he was not a role model.

"Just because I dunk a basketball doesn't mean I should raise your kids," Barkley said.

I agreed that just because we're athletes doesn't mean we're qualified to raise your children. But a part of me did not agree with that sentiment, because I thought we all played a role — parents, community leaders, and, yes, professional athletes. Whether we wanted to or not, we couldn't deny that we had an influence. In that sense, my stand made me a leader, because I knew there were people out there, young and old, who looked differently at America's history of oppression and injustice because of what I did. But was I a leader like a president or the head of a board? No, I didn't think so.

All this was part of an internal debate I was having at the time. Sometimes we want to talk ourselves out of thinking we are important. We are fighting against generations of conditioning. We don't want to look at ourselves as being leaders because society has always told us, "No, you can't be a leader, you always have to be led. You have to be *taught*. You can't possibly lead. You can't be original and unique."

Because I was now a voracious reader, I was aware of what happened to prominent athletes and people in other fields when they dared take a stand against the system. Those in power ultimately find a way to make them pay for bringing attention or embarrassment or controversy to the system, no matter how justified the attention and embarrassment may be. In the end, I knew it didn't matter if I was right or not. Somehow, some way, the NBA and those who profit from it would come after me.

One way that I tried to keep my sanity through it all was to read uplifting motivational quotes, passages, and articles. It was similar to how I used to wake up every morning when I was in elementary school, envisioning myself as a great basketball player. Now I was waking up and using the words of others to imagine myself emerging on the other side of this even stronger.

The Quran was the major source of power for me. The Quran instructs Muslims to speak out against injustice, even if it's against yourself. It says you should go public with this message and fear nothing but Allah. I was reading and reminding myself of this on a daily basis. I kept telling myself, *Life is short – what do you want your life to say for itself?* I wanted to be about more than a points-per-game average or a multimillion-dollar contract.

Once the season was over, I wasn't quite sure what would happen with the Nuggets. A part of me expected that they would get rid of me. After all, Bernie hadn't made me feel like he cared very much whether I was there. On the other hand, I thought Nuggets management might want to keep the nucleus of our squad together. Although we finished the 1995–1996 season with a disappointing 35–47 record (I would like to think it would have been closer to .500 if Bernie hadn't sent me home toward the end), we had made the playoffs the previous two seasons, including a huge first-round upset of the top-seeded Seattle SuperSonics in 1994. It was the first time an eight seed had beaten a top seed in a playoff series. Looking at how far the team had come and the strong relationships we players had with one another and with the city, I was thinking, *Nah, they ain't gonna break this team up. Buuuut, I wouldn't be surprised if they do.*

So, when word came from my agent that the Nuggets had traded me to the Sacramento Kings, I wasn't shocked or devastated. My response was more like a shrug. *Oh well.*

Clearly, getting me out of town was a bigger priority than keeping the squad intact. A few days before the start of training camp in October, I packed my bags and headed to Sacramento. I was hopeful that a new team would be a better situation for me, but to be honest, I was prepared for anything. I was also hoping that the trade would put the whole anthem controversy in my rearview mirror. I certainly didn't expect that it would still be following me five years later, when America woke up on September 11 and witnessed planes being flown into the World Trade Center. Soon after 9/11, I agreed to do an interview with HBO. Though I was speaking my truth, the interview was the match that incinerated the remaining threads of my NBA career.

I was brought into the world in Gulfport, Mississippi, by a midwife everybody called Miss King. The big event happened inside Miss King's house, in a section of the city known as "the Quarters." The Quarters wasn't exactly the high-rent district. I was told Miss King typically took payment for her services in many different forms, ranging from hard cash to a dozen eggs or even a chicken. It was 1969, not exactly the Dark Ages, but poor folk in Mississippi found ways to make it work. My mother never told me what she gave Miss King to deliver me; I don't know how many eggs I was worth.

On my birth certificate, on the line where it says "Father," mine was blank. Empty space. More than a half century later, the line is still blank. I have no idea who he was. That emptiness has been a source of pain for me throughout my life — a dull ache that sits in the pit of my stomach, persistent and confused. *Who was my father?*

My mother, Jacqueline Jackson, claimed I was always "different." "The child never crawled a day in his life," she said about me in a documentary called *By the Dawn's Early Light,* which was produced in 2002, the year before she died. "Once he was like seven months old, I said, 'I'll be right back.' I was in the bed, right? When I got back, he was walking. And I just — it freaked me out. I was screaming, you know. I said, 'What?' I said, 'Chris is walking!' This kid was different."

In those early years, I became all too familiar with another ache in my belly, next to the father ache — this one from hunger. My mother worked herself to exhaustion as a cook at the nearby Keesler Air Force Base in Biloxi, which was the World War II training ground for the famed Tuskegee Airmen. Though the job didn't pay a lot, it was at least a source of income that helped replenish the food supply.

But the Keesler job hadn't come easy. When she put in an application, for weeks my mom woke up at sunrise and, because she didn't have a car and couldn't afford public transportation, walked from Gulfport to the base in Biloxi — a distance of about eleven miles. At the base, she would sit quietly in the office, waiting for someone to call her name.

Days and weeks went by, and no one called her name. But she continued to get up each morning and make the trip. At one point, a white guy who was also applying for a job at Keesler drove by her on the road and recognized her as the woman sitting in the office. He started picking her up every day and driving her to the base. Finally, they had called out the name of everybody who was going to get a job. Her name hadn't been called. She had not a dime to her name and no other options that she could think of. They wanted to clear out the office and told everyone still waiting to leave. My mother went to the pay phone and pretended that she was making a phone call, but she didn't even have a quarter to put in the slot.

She heard a voice call out to her. "Ma'am?" She turned around and saw it was the white lady behind the desk. "Yes?" she answered. "Can I have a word with you?" the woman asked. She walked over to see what the woman wanted. "You come in here every single day and you sit patiently and you don't say a word. You really need this job, don't you?" She nodded. "Yes, ma'am, I do."

"Well, the job is yours. We're hiring you."

On that day she got hired as a dietitian, which I eventually discovered was a fancy word for a cook. It was a perfect illustration of this woman and her resilience. She didn't have a high school diploma, but she ached to take care of me and my two brothers. She wouldn't stop until she found a way.

But still, we were seriously poor. On many days, there just wasn't enough food for us. I was in elementary school and too young to understand what poverty was. Being poor is a state of mind that little children understand only in comparison to everybody around them. If everybody is poor, what you are is normal. Regular. But I *did* understand hunger. I knew it like I knew the crevices and cracks in the sidewalks of Avondale Circle, our apartment complex. I knew what it felt like to peer into the refrigerator and the cabinets in desperation, hoping to quiet the growl in my belly, but knowing my search wouldn't bear any more fruit than it did the last time I looked a few hours earlier.

I learned how to be creative. If there was a loaf of bread sitting in the cabinet, but nothing in the kitchen to put between the slices, I wouldn't let that stop me. I'd toast the bread, slather it with butter, and maybe sprinkle sugar on top to mix it up. If we had cinnamon, I'd make cinnamon toast.

Sometimes there wouldn't even be bread in the cabinet, but maybe there was ground coffee. I'd run the water in the sink until it got scorching hot, then mix hot water and coffee in a cup with plenty of sugar. I would drink three or four cups until my belly felt full. When the coffee can was empty, I'd mix sugar in the water and drink that. Poverty squeezes out this type of creativity for survival that only poor people can truly relate to.

My mother, like so many other Black mothers, had a way of making something out of nothing and putting a smile on your face. Buttered rice with salt and pepper was a meal by itself that didn't leave you disappointed. Beans and rice was one of our favorites. Breakfast foods were cheaper, so she would make cheese grits that would stick to our stomachs. On occasion, we would receive government cheese, which would come in this long cardboard-looking container and felt like cement and was almost just as tough to cut through. But we would make grilled cheese sandwiches or, other times, just eat the cheese by itself, which would certainly stick to our stomachs. Government cheese was surely worth the struggle.

During the school year, I looked forward to lunchtime because I knew at least I could count on the free lunch to fill my belly. Weekends were a different story, though. It's only in retrospect that I realize how tough it was for us. At the time, I assumed every child had to figure out ways to stop the growling in his stomach.

The beauty of living in a fertile, tropical place like Gulfport, where the average low temperature never drops below 60 degrees Fahrenheit, is that delicious fruits and nuts grow in abundance, often by the side of the road. This was good news indeed for a hungry little kid who liked to roam the streets. We moved to a neighborhood called Soria City, not far from Avondale, when I was about eight years old. There was a pear tree right near our house that was the source of many meals for me. Pecan trees were nearby, too; I'd scour the ground for pecans that were in an edible state. Dates, plums, blackberries—they were sprinkled all around the neighborhood. I'd make my shirt into a little basket and cart home as many as I could, eager to clean them so I could feast. If they actually made it home, I'd smother the berries in processed sugar to make a dessert for me and my little brother, Omar, who was seven years younger and my constant shadow at the time.

In the summer, my mother would take us along when she visited her sisters, my aunts Antoine and Sonja, in Bay St. Louis—about twenty minutes west along the coast toward New Orleans. My mom had an extensive support system that included aunts and uncles who were really influential in my upbringing. In Bay St. Louis, I would be amazed by the two huge fig trees in the yard of one of the neighbors because I wasn't used to seeing figs in our neighborhood. The figs were fleshy and delicious and acted almost like a food bank for the neighbors: you got what you needed and didn't even have to ask.

I didn't eat everything I came across. I knew what pears, plums, pecans, berries, and dates looked like. I also knew there were berries that looked red and inviting on the outside, but what was on the inside could kill you. I had an intense fear of death, probably fed by all my religious family members like my grandmother, aunts, and uncles always talking about it. I'd hear them say stuff like, "You better get your soul right or you gonna go to hell!"

I wasn't sure what it meant to get my soul "right," but I knew I didn't want to go to hell. I wasn't about to tempt the state of my soul by messing with a fruit or berry by the side of the road that I couldn't clearly identify.

Though I spent most of my time in a predominantly Black world when I was a kid, I noticed something strange about the way the people I loved acted when they were around white folks. As early as age seven, it jumped out at me every time I saw it—but I couldn't put my finger on exactly why I was unsettled by it. I just knew that I would walk away from witnessing the interactions with a weird sensation in the pit of my stomach.

My mother, my aunts, my uncles—all had a confident, even brash way about them when they were around family and friends. But their demeanors changed when they were around white folks. Their bodies would kind of slump over. Their diction would change. If they said something even remotely direct, they would say it softly, under their breath. They would become the physical embodiment of submissiveness. As soon as the person was gone, out of earshot, they'd become their brash selves once again. What was going on?

I eventually became well aware of Mississippi's painful and sordid racial history, but I didn't know anything about that as a second grader. All I knew was what I saw, and I didn't like it. Whatever was causing Black folks to behave this way, I wanted no part of it. They were surrendering to some invisible force that I wanted to understand—so that I could make sure it didn't sneak up on me. I was forming an aversion to submissiveness and suppression that would only grow over the years.

Neither did I have the vocabulary to express what I was feeling. Unfortunately, with too many Black families, racial tension and fear were subjects they would never discuss, particularly with their children. I was a respectful southern child, so I knew there were certain questions you just didn't ask, certain subjects you just didn't broach. I could close my eyes and picture the response I would have gotten if I tried to ask my grandmother why she was so timid around white people.

"Boy, who you think you talking to?!"

So, I just shut up and tried to figure it out myself. And it wasn't only around white people that I saw my mother's submissiveness emerge. It happened with some Black people, too—anyone she believed to have some type of authority over her. I guess this was a survival instinct honed by years of life in Mississippi.

On one particular occasion, I decided I had had enough; I had to do something about it. She was "dating" a man who lived nearby—a man who was married to someone else. When I was growing up, it wasn't uncommon for dudes to be married to one woman and have another woman up the street. My mother was the woman up the street. Her whole personality would change when he came over, and her mannerisms would become much more deferential, catering to this guy. I knew how she normally was, so it was quite noticeable to me. I felt like it was demeaning for her to act this way.

One day when I was in fifth grade, I was lying in bed when I heard the sound of my mother crying on the front steps of our place in Soria City. There is perhaps no sound as dramatically disturbing to a little kid as the sound of his mother crying. I rushed outside to see what was the matter. She was out there with her best friend, Gail. The married man was standing in the dirt by the edge of the porch.

He was swaying like he was drunk. My mother was looking at him with tears streaming down her face.

I knew right away that whatever was wrong with her, he was the cause of it. I looked at her and her tears, then I looked out at him, standing in the yard. I felt a pulse of anger throbbing in my head. Without a word, I turned and went back into the house. I located the thick wooden Louisville Slugger baseball bat we kept in the house. Clutching the bat in my hands, I walked back outside and moved toward this guy. He was a lot bigger than me, but I was still standing on the porch, so I towered over him. I was so angry I was no longer in control of my actions. I was determined to hit this dude upside the head for making my mother cry.

"Boy, what you doin'?!" My mother's eyes were wide as she shouted at me. "Put that damn bat back!" she said angrily.

I was always one to listen to my mother. But in this case, I was so angry I stood there and glared at the dude. A voice in my head was urging me to swing the bat at his head, but the voice of reason won out.

"Dammit, boy, didn't I tell you . . . ?!"

I finally turned around and looked at my mother. I saw that she meant business. I turned back toward her "boyfriend." Our eyes locked. Even though he was clearly drunk, I saw his eyes widen just a bit. We had made some sort of connection. I could peer into his head and read his thoughts: *This little nigga is for real.*

I'm not sure how their relationship was altered by that day, but I know after that I never saw him do anything to my mother to make her cry again.

CHAPTER 3

W hen I was in second or third grade, I began to have
strange, inexplicable "episodes" where I momentarily blacked out.
Something was happening with my brain that I didn't understand.
My mind would go blank, like I drifted out of full consciousness,
going somewhere else — sometimes right in the middle of an activity.
I mostly started noticing it in fourth grade, though in retrospect I
think the episodes began happening earlier than that. For example,
the painful incident with the ants.

I was sitting behind a section of bushes one day where I was
being watched by my grandmother, perhaps when I was five or six.
I didn't realize that I was sitting right on top of a large ant bed — that
is, until I got up and the ants all over my body started biting me.
I yelled as I ran to my grandmother for help. She scooped me up,
brought me inside, and dumped me in the bathtub after stripping
off my clothes. She filled the tub with water and dumped in a jug of
stinky vinegar. I felt the stinging all over my body as I soaked in the
water and vinegar, which definitely helped with the pain.

I felt good enough to go back outside a little while later.
Believe it or not, I walked back behind the bushes, almost like I was
in a trance, and sat right back in the same bed of ants. And once
again, the ants attacked me, biting me all over. I have no idea what
was going through my head, if anything. When my grandmother
looked at me like I was crazy, I couldn't explain to her what had
happened. But in retrospect, I think I had one of my blackout spells.

My mother started to notice that I would zone out at times,
putting me in a state where I was oblivious to everything around

me. I suppose it looked like I was falling asleep, because my mother would smack me upside the head when it happened.

"What did I just tell you to do?! You over here going to sleep!" she said more than once. I looked at her in confusion. "Mom, I wasn't sleeping," I said. "But I'm looking right at you," she said. "I see you. You tellin' me I'm lying?" Back and forth we'd go, neither one of us understanding what was happening.

One time I was walking on my hands, playing around with friends. But apparently, I blacked out while I was upside down. I landed on my head and knocked myself out. When I woke up, I saw my friends looking down at me with big round eyes. They had been shaking me, wondering what happened. I reached up and felt an enormous lump on my head.

On another occasion, I blacked out in the middle of a boxing match in the Soria City courtyard with a guy named Benny McGee. As we squared off against each other, I blacked out for just a beat, and when I came back, he had a shocked look on his face. I wasn't as concerned as he was; I put up my hands to continue boxing. "Chris, man, you blacked out!" one of my friends said. "Benny punched you dead in your jaw!"

Sitting in class was one of my biggest challenges. Having conversations with myself to try to sit still and be invisible while my body was screaming to be noticed was mentally, physically, and emotionally draining. It's almost impossible to learn, because you can't truly hear what's being said on account of trying to stay still and not end up being the target of jokes. It was like my brain had a will of its own; I couldn't control what my mind wanted to focus on. I noticed that sometimes when I read a passage, my mind would be fighting with me. The words needed to roll off my lips, and I had to comprehend them at the same time, otherwise I had to go over the sentences again and again. As a result, it might take me ten minutes or more to read a page and understand what I just read. At the same time, I would have difficulty controlling my body and even my face as I sat at the hard wooden desk, so much so that it would be next to impossible at times to concentrate on what the teacher was saying. These struggles between my brain and my body got harder and harder, affecting the quality of my work. School became an increasingly uncomfortable place for me.

At its worst, this mind control problem became an issue for me even with something as basic as shutting a door. I'd shut it, then my mind would tell me to open it and shut it again because something just wasn't right about the way I'd shut it. I'd do it again, but my mind still wouldn't like the way I did it. I might open and shut the door five or six times before my mind let me walk away.

On some mornings, it would take me a half hour or more to get dressed for school because my socks felt uncomfortable or my shirt didn't fit quite right. I would do it over and over, a prisoner of my mind's compulsive need to have everything feel perfect before it would let me move on to the next thing.

Homework was another challenge. I might have to write out the answer to a question numerous times until my mind was convinced that my answer was perfect. This could go on for a long time. Every imperfection was exacerbated, enlarged in my mind, until I couldn't think about anything else.

In effect, my mind was always telling me, *Chris, if you don't make me feel comfortable, I will make your life hell. You must satisfy me first!*

When my eyes popped open in the morning, I would feel a sense of dread, wondering how difficult my mind would be to negotiate with on this particular day. I would tell myself, *Okay, this is a new day. I'm gonna get through this day without hesitation. I'm not going to let this thing take control of me.*

I would take a deep breath, push back the covers, and step out of bed. *Bam!* Almost immediately, my mind would tell me I had to repeat the process over again because it didn't feel right.

My body was always in constant movement, despite my best efforts to stop it. Perpetual ants in my pants. The moving would be a persistent worry for me. I knew that if I didn't control it, my face could twitch and contort in a very noticeable way, which I found to be terribly embarrassing. But the effort to fight the twitching made it worse, turning me into a ball of tension, praying I could keep it under control.

There were times when I would have a tic so violent that my arm would fly out uncontrollably and I'd fear that I had dislocated my elbow. Or my head would twitch so hard that I would get a stabbing pain in my neck and it'd feel like my brain was hitting my skull. I'd look in the mirror and watch myself have these uncontrollable twitches, right there in front of my face, and wonder, *What's wrong with me?* I spent so much time and energy trying to control this stuff, especially when I was around other people.

Uncontrollable tics and twitches aren't going to go unnoticed by other kids. It made me different. *Weird.* Little kids can be some cruel little monsters; I was the object of plenty of ridicule. I didn't like it, but I knew that the worst thing I could do was show how much it bothered me. Kids smell fear and weakness like a shark sensing blood in the water. If I looked like I was hurt by the taunts, they were just going to come at me harder. Sometimes I would try to fire back some kind of insult in response, but I was never quick-witted like that. I preferred to keep a low profile with that stuff. We called it "janking," trading insults back and forth. I think every Black neighborhood probably has its own terminology. Janking was never my strong suit.

I noticed that other dudes seemed to be more likely to make an issue of my tics around girls, especially if they sensed that a girl might like me more. I would just stare at them, making a mental note: *Wait until P.E. Just wait. I'll get you back when we're playing sports. I'm going to make you look ridiculous.*

My mother observed my struggles and eventually knew something was wrong. She wasn't a passive observer; she tried to get me help. She brought me to several local doctors in Gulfport, but they were unable to diagnose what was going on with me. When I think back on it now, I'm somewhat disturbed that I went so long suffering with this condition without anybody being able to put a finger on what was wrong. I didn't get a name for it until I was seventeen years old: Tourette syndrome. That's how long it took for a medical professional to say those two words to me. When I started researching the condition, I found that it was first named in 1885 by the French neurologist and neuropsychiatrist Georges Gilles de la Tourette, who described nine cases of the syndrome and its many different symptoms while working at the Salpêtrière Hospital in Paris. But because the symptoms are so varied, many children can go a long time before a doctor gives them a proper diagnosis. It usually begins between the ages of five and seven and is most commonly characterized by many tics and twitches. Only 10 to 15 percent of individuals with Tourette have the swearing tic (coprolalia), where they have outbursts of uncontrollable swearing—the symptom that has gotten the most media attention. Though sometimes words came out of my mouth with more force than I intended, I've never experienced the swearing.

I was most startled to learn that, according to some experts, Tourette affects as many as 1 percent of young people between the ages of five and eighteen across the globe, though most will go undiagnosed. Interestingly, studies suggest it is much less common among African Americans and almost nonexistent among sub-Saharan

Africans, for reasons that aren't clear. Certainly, more study is needed to figure out why.

I was still in elementary school the first time my mother brought me to a doctor, probably about nine or ten years old. After he poked around for a bit, the doctor made his diagnosis: "You have habits," he said. "They come and they go."

At least I had a word for it. *Habits*. When people asked me what was wrong with me, why I twitched so much, I would respond, "Oh, I just have habits."

The doctor even gave me "medicine" to fix it: these giant orange horse pills with some sort of gel inside. I didn't know it at the time, but the pills were just placebos. I hated those things; they were so big they would make me gag. And they were useless in stopping the twitching and my obsessive-compulsive behavior. That probably would have been the most useful aspect of a real diagnosis—an explanation for the obsessive-compulsive behavior that nearly drove me mad for most of my childhood.

I used to hide the giant pills inside these big cinder blocks that were in the back of the house we were renting at the time. We rented the house for $200 a month from a guy named Mr. Taylor. In the rear of the house, where the washer and dryer were located, Mr. Taylor had started to build additional rooms but had never finished the job, leaving walls of exposed cinder blocks that provided me with a perfect hiding place. I wanted my mother to think I was taking them every day, so I would stash the daily pill in the cinder block instead of down my throat.

In another attempt to figure out what was wrong with me, my mother brought me to a hospital in Gulfport. I remember a white lady putting EEG sensors on my head with this white paste. Afterward, she told me that I had to stay awake for twenty-four hours, though she never explained why. I struggled to keep from drifting off in the wee

hours that night. After the probing, they weren't able to tell us anything more than what we already knew. *Habits.*

"When I first noticed my son had . . . Tourette's, he would
actually just irritate me, right?" my mother said in the documentary.
"Open—open-closing, open-closing the refrigerator door—open. I
was just, 'Shut the door and let it be.' And then he'd tie his shoes and
he'd take 'em and unlace them and tie 'em again, and I said, 'You're
driving me nuts.' I didn't know he had that problem. And once I
realized it, it made me cry. I cried a many days. I said, 'I'm hollering
at my son for something he couldn't control.'"

In the midst of my struggles with Tourette, there was a reason
I wasn't the object of even more ridicule: sports. I had been identified
as a superior athlete in fourth grade, which was when the "habits"
were most intense. Even if many of the people around me were
inclined to think something was wrong, my athletic abilities probably made the adults less likely to speak up and the kids less likely
to tease me. After all, if this kid could do all *that* on the court or the
field, how much of a hindrance could the twitching possibly be?

CHAPTER 4

In the town of Gulfport, sports was king when I was growing up. Still is. Among my little circle of friends, play was just about all we did. Football. Baseball. Basketball. We did it all. There were a few very rudimentary versions of video games that could keep us entertained, although my friends and I didn't exactly have the funds for an Atari. Instead, we were outside all day, every day. Sports was an escape from whatever might be missing back in our homes.

For me, sports was something more: a way out. I recognized early on that it was a path for me. If I worked hard enough, I could follow the example of my idol, Dr. J, and find the riches that I felt Mississippi could never offer me. Of course, just about every other little boy in America dreams of becoming a professional athlete and getting rich and famous. Especially little boys in poor neighborhoods. But for me, it was many levels beyond that. It wasn't a dream, per se. It was a conviction.

By third grade I knew I had exceptional athletic gifts. When you're running and jumping with your friends, it doesn't take long to discover who can run faster and jump higher than everybody else. I had fast-twitch muscles, innate body control, and quickness, which allowed me the opportunity to dominate in whatever sport we might be playing. When we played sandlot football, no matter the position—quarterback, wide receiver—I would stand out.

With football, I needed extra motivation to get inspired. I needed to get pissed off, to get hit, in order for my competitive juices to be unleashed. In addition, football and Tourette didn't coexist well. All that equipment, all the adjusting and tugging, maaaan,

I'd probably not make it out of the locker room until the first half was over, trying to get everything to feel just right. And then there was basketball. My connection to that big round ball was immediate. Intense. I fell in love right away.

As a kid, I decided I needed to become the best basketball player on the face of the Earth. Not second best. Not really good. THE BEST. "You can only be *one* of the best!" my cousin Robin would say to me during our many arguments on the subject. "No! I want to be *the* best. Not just *one* of the best," I'd say. "*THE* best!"

In fourth grade, I started committing myself to a workout routine that soon became a part of who I am. To call it "grueling" or "intense" is a serious understatement. I had locked in on the goal of getting to the NBA, so I decided that I would push myself until I got there. Starting at age nine, I would wake up every morning at 4:00 A.M. to be on the basketball court around the corner by 5:00 A.M. For years, my mother had no idea I was doing this. I sensed that she would think it was too extreme, too dangerous, too much. I would wait until she left for her job at the Air Force base, where she had to report by 5:00 A.M.

I was out the door as soon as I heard her car drive off. It didn't matter if the sky was raging with thunder and lightning or if it was cold outside. I wasn't going to be deterred. It's still very dark at 4:30 or 4:45 A.M. I didn't care. My mindset was that I had no choice because this was the only way I was going to get out of Gulfport and escape the hardships of poverty. I had to do more than anybody else was doing. That's why I say my commitment was many levels beyond what other little boys were doing in elementary school.

I wasn't a particularly tall kid at the time. My mother wasn't tall, either. Since I didn't know who my father was, I had no idea whether I would grow to a decent NBA height. My role model and inspiration, Dr. J, was a long, elegant 6'7". It seemed unlikely I would come anywhere close to that, so I concluded that I would have to be exceptional, dramatically so, to overcome whatever I wasn't going to get in height.

I never saw academics as my path out of poverty. No one ever told me that school could make me rich. I was told that you go to school so that you can graduate and get a good job. Well, I didn't want just a *good* job. I wanted to be rich. Wealthy. And the people I saw with wealth on TV were actors, entertainers, and athletes. Even the doctors and the lawyers who I was aware of in Gulfport weren't rich. That wasn't what I wanted. I could not see a connection between education and wealth at that age, at least not for a Black person. My mother had gone to school only up to the eighth grade. Nobody in my family had gone to college. Who was going to teach me the importance of education? The height of my mother's aspirations for me was to get a high school diploma.

Besides, with Tourette, school was painful for me anyway, a place where I found very little success. I went to school only because I saw it as the necessary path to the NBA. It was a transition. When guys told me in high school, "Look, all you need is a C to play," I was going to shoot for that C, the bare minimum. Enough to get by. I realized that I could memorize my way through, take enough in so that I could spit it out when necessary. As a result, I never actually learned anything. I would literally tell myself, *Okay, I'm going to study this, this, and this so that I can pass the test.* But I was never taught how to be a critical thinker. I didn't grow up in that family where we were taught critical-thinking and problem-solving skills, where there were books all around the house.

As early as fourth grade, I decided it was basketball or death. Basketball or poverty and suffering. If I didn't make it in basketball, I didn't know what my life would look like, but I thought it would be bleak. Ugly. I woke every morning with my heart pounding hard, terrified that I was going to fail and wind up on the street or toiling away in some dead-end job. I had to make it happen on the court because it was all I had.

I spent a lot of time playing with guys who were much older than me, which did a lot for building my confidence. I'd spend hours playing 21 with Boo Cooper, Mitchell Quince, Tony, Dan, and Spencer, who were all in high school when I was just a fourth grader. I started building a reputation.

It all began one day when they were picking teams for a full-court run, and Boo looked in my direction. Boo was a popular guy, known on the streets for being a tough but quality dude, as well as for his abilities at boxing and basketball. "I got Chris," he said, pointing at me.

All eyes turned to me, just a little kid, the first pick to play with high school dudes. Nobody expressed surprise. I believe they saw something in me and wanted me to succeed. They would give me the "rock" and encourage me time and again to go at whoever was guarding me. I put in some serious work that day, hitting shots from all over. *Pop! Pop! Pop!*

After the game, in what would become somewhat of a ritual, Mitchell grabbed me. "Come on, boy," he said, handing me the ball. "Let's go." That was my cue to engage in some intense workouts with Mitchell, who towered over me at 6'2". Mitchell would deliberately be overly physical with me, using his size to push me around. He was making me tough, able to withstand punishment and not let it slow me down.

One day when I was on the court playing with my brother David, who was three years older, and his best friend, Dave Warren, outside of Central Elementary School, I heard a voice call out to me. "Chris! Come here!" I looked up and saw the voice belonged to a woman we called Miss Cookie; her real name was Oceletta. She had a son, Tony, who was a good athlete, and a daughter, Michelle, who was a skilled athlete, and cheerleader, so she was a familiar figure at sporting events around town. I didn't even know she had been watching us play.

In the South, when an older person tells you to "come here," you come. And besides, Miss Cookie was a large, strong-natured woman — the type of woman Tyler Perry would later channel with Madea. I wasn't about to defy Miss Cookie. She didn't play.

"Yes, ma'am?" I said.

"Go in there and try out," she said.

"Huh?" I had no idea what she was talking about.

"They're having fourth grade basketball tryouts in the gym right now," she said. "You get in there and try out for the team."

"Well, Miss Cookie, you're going to have to ask my mama first," I said.

She dismissed that with a wave of her hand. "Don't worry about that," she said. "I'll talk to your mama. Go in there and try out!"

I nodded. "Yes, ma'am."

I went into the gym and saw a bunch of my peers shooting around. *Why didn't I know about this?* The coach, a white man, finally told me to get on the court. At this point, all my basketball experience consisted of playground ball, mostly games of 21 and two-on-two. I didn't know a thing about organized team basketball. All I knew was, when you get the ball, you try to score by any means possible — and whoever scores the most wins, right? Every time I got the ball, I zoomed through and around the opposition, each time putting the ball in the basket. Over and over again. *Bam! Bam! Bam!* Scoring at will.

After the tryout was over, the coach announced who had made the team. I was so happy to hear my name. As we were about to leave, the coach pulled me aside. "Hey, son," he said with a slight chuckle. "You gonna have to learn how to pass."

Our first game was at a gym called Gaston Hewes Recreation Facility. Before we were about to leave the bathroom—which served as our locker room—and take the court, I was nervous and clueless. I pulled aside a kid I had befriended named Theron Gross, who had played before. "Hey, man, like what do we do when we go out?" I asked him. "What happens?"

He looked at me closely, perhaps unsure exactly what I was asking him at first. He patted me on the shoulder and said, "Don't worry, man, just follow me."

I didn't know how a game would feel. I was nervous I might make a fool of myself. Once the game started, my jitters disappeared as soon as I got the ball the first time. I knew what to do with the ball in my hands: score. And that's what I did. A lot.

Despite his comment to me that I needed to learn how to pass, the coach at one point gave the team pretty simple instructions: "Give Chris the ball and move out of the way."

I scored 21 points in my first organized game. That was a large percentage of the team's total points. I felt unbelievably excited walking off the court. It was better than I even imagined it would be. There was no question about it—this was *for real* what I wanted to do with my life. At that moment, basketball was officially elevated in my mind above all the other sports. My vision of making it to the NBA had become a lot more believable. All I had to do was put in the work—more work than any other kid in the United States.

CHAPTER 5

My early-morning workouts were so intense, so extreme, that when I got on the court against other guys, things were ridiculously easy for me. During those early mornings, I was not only competing against my imagination; I was doing battle with Tourette. It had its own ravenous appetite, always looking to be fed. If I didn't feed it, it would take over my mind and make my life miserable. In effect, I was a slave to the syndrome.

I somehow recognized, even in fourth, fifth, and sixth grade, that learning how to do things in unorthodox ways would give me an advantage, make me unpredictable. If everybody is taught to always shoot off the left foot when driving to the right, what would happen if I sometimes shot off the right foot, or shot with my left hand? No one would expect it. When you make unpredictability a pattern, you become a problem for your opponents. That became one of my fundamental beliefs. Much of it was driven by my suspicion that I was going to be small. I knew I had to be exceptional, because if a team had to choose between me and a dude who's 6'5", and we pretty much do the same stuff, who do you think they're going with? They're going to think that other guy can guard bigger guys, get more rebounds. My mission was to give them pause, make them think, *Yeah, I know he's shorter, but dang, this kid can play.*

I also had that Mississippi chip on my shoulder, something that a lot of us carry around with us, thinking we don't get as much respect because of where we're from. There just weren't a lot of big names in the sports world from Mississippi—at least names I was familiar with. I knew about Walter Payton. The list of elite athletes in my mind pretty much ended there when I was in elementary school. I was always hearing about these bad dudes from the big cities. Those were the thoughts bouncing around my head during my early morning workouts — that this Mississippi kid was gonna be going up against guards from New York City, Philly, Chicago. Even my role model, Dr. J, hailed from New York, though in his case it was Long Island, not New York City. From the beginning, I had something to prove to the world.

But the obsession with basketball came at a steep price: I failed fourth grade and got held behind. It was painfully embarrassing. Somehow, I didn't see it coming, though I should have because I stopped paying any real attention to my schoolwork. It was like my mind didn't have enough room to fit in basketball and school. I would do my work in class, but when I got home, I pushed all school matters to the side to focus on basketball. Homework that year was a foreign concept to me.

When the teacher handed me my report card toward the end of the school year, I couldn't believe what I saw: every single grade was a big blinking U. *Unsatisfactory.*

I swallowed hard and looked around, hoping nobody saw it. Luckily, everybody was too busy scanning their own report cards.

I was scared to death to bring that report card home to my mother. I knew she would lose it. So, I held on to it for several days. Every time I looked at my book bag, it felt like the report card was staring back out at me, asking, *"What you gonna do, Chris?"*

My teacher reminded me more than once that I needed to get the report card signed and returned. A sense of dread just sat in my stomach, never going away.

After a few days, one morning I noticed that my mother seemed to be in an especially good mood while driving me to school. She was singing along with the music and appeared to be full of joy. If I had been an adult, I might have picked a different time, not wanting to ruin her mood. But fourth graders don't think that way. It was all about me. I figured this was the best time to minimize the damage.

She stopped the car in front of the school and looked over at me with a cheery smile.

"Ma, I got something to tell you," I said.

"What, baby?" she responded, still smiling.

I already had my hand inside my bag, on the report card. I pulled it out and handed it to her. Then I braced myself. Her entire face transformed, like someone had flipped a switch. She looked away for a second. I could see her jaw tense; she was grinding her teeth together. She turned back to me, her eyes ablaze.

"When you get home, I'm gonna whup your muthafuckin' ass!" she said. When she got mad, just about every curse word in the English language might fly out of her mouth.

I quickly slid out of the car, just in case she decided to begin the whupping right there in front of Central Elementary School. I was useless that entire day, sitting at my desk, staring at the teacher, my mind envisioning the beating I was going to get later. I had gotten pretty severe beatings for infractions a lot less serious than all U's on my report card. I knew she would be coming at me like Wonder Woman.

She gave it to me good that night. Afterward, I ran into my room, sobbing. A few minutes later, she entered my room. This was part of the ritual: after the beating, she always wanted to come and deliver the same old speech.

"Baby, you know I love you," she said. "I whup you because I love you."

One time a few years later, when she gave me her little post-whupping speech, I had to say something.

"Ma, I hear you," I said, between sniffles as I looked at her. "But you be whupping me too hard." I didn't say it, but I was thinking, *This doesn't feel like love. Not to me. If it is, I don't want no part of it.*

As an adult, even though I beat my kids in the beginning, I changed. I decided that there were other ways than physical force I wanted to pursue to discipline and teach my children. When I came to that realization, I apologized to them for the times I had laid my hands on them.

In some ways the fear of getting a whupping from my mother did act as a deterrent when I was young. Well, maybe not quite a deterrent. It might not have stopped me from doing things I shouldn't have been doing, but the fear did serve as a voice in my head, letting me know I better not get caught. For instance, when I would steal food to quiet the growling in my belly, I would be terrified, thinking about what she would do to me if she found out.

I wasn't stealing just to be stealing. I was stealing because I was starving. When I walked home from the courts outside Central Elementary, if I was especially hungry after playing, I couldn't resist making a slight detour and heading to the Jitney Jungle supermarket. My first stop was usually the produce section, where I would grab a handful of grapes to snack on right away to quiet the grumbling. As I munched on the grapes, I headed for the canned meats and beans aisle. I would already be nearly salivating when I saw my prey: Vienna sausages, rows and rows of the little cans, neatly lined up. Before I struck, I looked around several times, making sure I was alone in the aisle. I would slide two or three cans down into my drawers under my shorts. Then I'd head for the exit. I tried to pretend that I had come there to buy something and had abruptly changed my mind. I wasn't no Denzel Washington, but I thought my act was believable. Because the cans made my shorts bulge out way too much, I would put the ball in front of my privates like a shield and do a fingertip drill as I walked, tapping the ball back and forth between my right and left hands. When I got about a block away, I'd open the cans and feast on the sausages on the way home. They were a perfect postgame snack.

Once, I almost got caught. Somebody came around the corner into the aisle just as I was about to slide the cans down south. My heart was pounding so hard I thought I was having a heart attack. I'm not even sure the person worked in the store. I hurried up and made my getaway — after, of course, taking what I had gone there for. As I walked away from the store, I thought about my mom wearing me out with a switch or a cord. *Whew! That was way too close.*

Though it would be a couple more years before she actually came to a game to see me play, my mother recognized my obsession early on, even if she didn't always like it.

"He was always out there with that ball," she said in the documentary. "Never did do no homework. He would come in, he would sit down and eat, put the ball right there by the table. I said, 'What is with this ball?' This was me, this was my reaction: 'You about to drive me crazy with this ball,' sitting down there by the bed. He gets through eating, he'd get up, he'd take the ball, and he'd leave. He go get in the tub, he got the ball. Jesus! So I never thought nothing about the ball. I said, 'He just love a ball, that's it.'"

In those first couple of years of organized basketball during elementary school, I rose above the competition right away. In one game, we lost 45–43, and I had 42 of our 43 points. Another game we lost 42–36 and I had all 36. I started to get invited to play in summer leagues, to play against more elevated competition. But my dominance continued. I'm embarrassed to say that I started listening a bit too much to the things people were saying about me. I had an unforgettable encounter after a pickup game on the playground that came at just the right time. There's nothing wrong with believing in yourself, but there's a fine line between being confident and cocky. I had definitely crossed that line.

During the game, I was putting in work. I was playing against dudes who were a lot older and bigger than me, and they were having trouble stopping me. I got caught up in the excitement, especially hearing the comments I was getting from the court spectators. There was a guy guarding me who was nearly twice my age and well over six feet. If he wasn't out of high school yet, he was about to be. He was having a difficult time stopping me. And the guys around the court were letting him hear it.

"Put it on him, young fella!"

"Oooh, you see what he did?!"

I got caught up in the hype. Instead of controlling my emotions, I started talking trash to him, telling him that he couldn't guard me. He was already mad that I was a little kid giving him the business, puncturing his pride. Now I was gonna try to double his embarrassment on top of it? This dude wasn't having it.

"Ah, shut up, man!" he yelled at me.

But I didn't stop. I said something else after I scored on him. I could see his face: dude was about to explode. There wasn't much danger of a physical confrontation—I was way too little for him to gain anything by beating me up.

The game took place on the other side of Soria City, blocks from my house. When it ended and I began walking home, he started walking in the same direction. It was obvious his anger had spilled off the court and he had to get something off his chest. He needed to tell me what he thought of me. He cursed me out like I've never been cursed out before or since.

"You son of a bitch!" he yelled. "You arrogant asshole, you need to learn humility! Everyone has their day, and what goes around comes around."

I tried to say something back to him, but my heart wasn't in it. "Oh, man, shut up!" I said. "You don't know me! Forget you!"

But the words coming out of my mouth were only to camouflage how devastated I was by what he had said to me. I was so demoralized and hurt that I had turned into a person that I never wanted to be: an arrogant loudmouth. That encounter was lifesaving for me. I wish I could remember who that guy was so I can track him down and thank him for what he did. I was so teeth-clenching mad at myself for how I acted during the game, I vowed to never do something like that again. I decided from that moment forward to always let my actions speak for me, to carry myself with humility and respect for others. To always remind myself that no matter how many shots were falling, there was always room for improvement. To always be grateful but never satisfied. To stay humble and hungry.

Those became the principles I would live by. Amazingly, when I started carrying myself with humility, all kinds of doors started swinging open for me. My star skyrocketed.

Well, I soared in basketball, but I was very much still earthbound when it came to academic matters. I was seriously struggling to concentrate in school, and it was noticed by my teachers. My Tourette still hadn't been diagnosed. It was taking me forever to read through passages because I had to keep going back over the material again and again until it felt *right*. It would have been difficult for me to explain to people, even my teachers, why reading took so long and why my comprehension suffered so much. I just didn't have the words to describe what was going on in my brain. To the educators at the school, clearly I was "slow."

One day when I was in seventh grade, my mother got summoned to the school to meet with a high-level African-American administrator. I had no idea what the meeting was about as I sat next to my mother on the other side of his desk.

"Miss Jackson, we think your son needs to be moved to a special education class," he said.

I looked at my mother, waiting for her to object. But she didn't. She uttered a few words but no objections.

My eyes bulged. She hadn't put up any kind of fight on my behalf. As I said, my mother had only an eighth grade education; I felt this was another example of her showing too much deference in the presence of authority figures. I was already a well-known athlete by this point, but I knew right away that no matter how great a basketball player I was, I would immediately become the dummy in the eyes of my peers. The ridicule would be harsh. I thought about the line that the special education students had to walk in, moving down the hall single file while the rest of the school watched them. The image was horrifying. They even had their own little building where they were taught.

"I know sometimes it takes me longer to read stuff," I said. "But I don't need to be in special ed! Please, Mom, don't let them do this."

The principal just stared back at me with a sad look on his face. As I glared at him, I knew that my life was about to radically change.

"Mom, no offense to people who need this, but I don't need special ed," I said. But she didn't have it in her to advocate on my behalf.

When I got moved to the special education class, I was constantly trying to figure out how to walk near the other kids without looking like I was in the special education line. Every time we left the classroom, I felt embarrassed and humiliated.

Inside the classroom, I quickly realized I had lucked out. My teacher, a white guy whose name I don't remember, was very empathetic. He told us, "Listen, if you guys can show me you don't belong, I'll get you out of here."

I took his words to heart. This was my chance to escape. For the next month or so, I buckled down. I pushed myself to move more quickly, to absorb more material.

One day the teacher came over to me. "Hey, man," he said. "You don't belong in this class."

Elation coursed through my body. I was going back.

"No offense, but that's what I been trying to tell you," I said.

CHAPTER 6

I t was around middle school when I began to discover the large ecosystem of youth basketball that existed outside of the school setting. Primarily it was represented by the Amateur Athletic Union (AAU) and by a network of basketball camps — both were proving grounds where the most promising players would compete and constantly be evaluated by adults, many with vested interests in the development of these talented players.

One of the teams that I dominated during a game in fifth grade happened to be coached by a man named Eddie Miller, a white attorney who also coached the AAU team for which his son, Owen, played. Miller, who would eventually become my first sports agent, asked me to play for his AAU team during the summer after sixth grade. Free hamburgers, free sneakers, exciting trips in the area — I liked AAU right away. Playing against more skilled opponents gave me immediate opportunities to assess whether I was getting better. I saw that with my intense early-morning workouts — on weekends during the school year and every day during the summer — I was making huge leaps in my skill set. I would work on the strength of my wrist by lying on my back and flicking up to "shoot" the ball straight in the air. I made a habit of doing this. Soon, I was nailing threes from well behind the line, shooting a clean jumper with my wrist while a lot of other elementary school players were still flinging it from the hip. The wrist strength gave me a great advantage because I could get my shot up quickly, even if I was closely guarded.

Before AAU, while I was in elementary school, I had the opportunity to go to a camp led by the legendary coach of Gulfport High School, Bert Jenkins. Coach Jenkins was the winningest coach in the state of Mississippi and had won seven state championships by the time he retired. One of his teams went 40–0 and is still considered the best high school team in Mississippi history (I wasn't on that team).

I knew Coach Jenkins had his eye on me, and I was excited about playing for him when I left junior high after ninth grade. He was a meticulous, no-nonsense coach whose teams were known for their discipline. I thought it was a system that would work very well for me. Even though I was trying to be unorthodox and unpredictable in how I created shots, I was always very disciplined. Even at that age, I learned that the way you play during practice influences what the coaches will let you get away with in the game. If they see you taking unorthodox shots in practice, trying unusual moves, their eyes get used to seeing you do it. Their souls become accepting of it, even if they don't realize it's happening. They see you doing fall-aways and leaners and turn-arounds, see you making them. So, when game time comes and you try one of these moves, they're going to be a lot less likely to yell at you like they might with somebody else. You have to train your coaches. At every level I've played, I would be in the gym before practice, attempting all kinds of unusual shots, knowing that the coach was often watching me. Over time, the coach develops trust in your game—no matter how much of your game might be outside of his normal comfort zone.

In junior high, I was average height, similar to most of the other boys my age, still well under six feet but inching closer. I developed a workout regimen that I thought would maximize my jumping skills, in case I didn't grow much more. I would jump up on and down from porches, run in combat boots, run on the beach (distance and sprints), squat and jump from a standing position, or do interval jumps off the right leg and then the left. Those probably looked especially stupid to a spectator, particularly when I did them up and down the street, but I didn't care. I was preparing for my future. In seventh grade, when I was about 5'9", I decided to jump up at the end of gym class and see how close I could get to the rim. I was wearing jeans at the time, but I still was able to grab the rim. With ease. *Oh my.*

I felt an excitement start bubbling up. *Does this mean what I think it does?* To prove it wasn't a fluke, I casually walked up and jumped once again. *Boom!* I grabbed the rim again, just as easily.

As soon as I could, I got back on a court to see if it was going to happen. I moved toward the rack with the ball, I leaped . . . and I flushed it. I dunked the ball with both hands on the first try, leaping off both feet. It was crazy. I was so thrilled, I could hardly contain my excitement.

By the time I got to eighth grade, I was capable of putting on a dunk exhibition: double-pump dunks, dunking after putting the ball between my legs. For those who've never done it, there are few things that rival the excitement of discovering that you are capable of dunking a basketball. Although I was dunking in practice all the time, I still was hesitant to try it in a game. Even on breakaways after a steal, when there was nobody around me, I would just do a customary layup.

It wasn't until ninth grade that I finally worked up the nerve to dunk in a game. I was going up against a kid named Litterial Green, a talented guard who was a year younger than me. Litterial went on to become the leading scorer in University of Georgia history and played for many years in the NBA, but in 1985, we were just two young teenagers battling for court dominance. His team was inbounding the ball when I deflected the pass and headed toward the hoop with the ball. When I took off, I was fully intending to just lay it in. But as I rose toward the rim, I realized at the last second just how high I was. On a whim, I threw it down. By the time I landed, the gym had already exploded. I soaked in the frenzied crowd noise.

Oh yeah, I could get used to this. From that moment on, I was trying to throw it down any chance I had during a game. I was like a young lion tasting human blood for the first time.

As I became more well-known around the city, folks in my neighborhood looked out for me in interesting ways. They knew I was likely headed for big things; they made sure I didn't get caught up in any foolishness. While Gulfport was a smaller city and didn't have the same level of street danger as cities like New York and Chicago, it still was a good idea to be on high alert when you left the house. We had drugs, we had prostitution, we had street fights. Occasionally we'd hear about somebody getting shot. It wasn't overrun by street crime, but it had the same ills as any ghetto in the United States.

When I played organized games, I often saw people looking at me harder than usual. They wouldn't necessarily be pointing, but they'd be whispering. As soon as the game started, I knew all eyes would be on me. Everybody would be telling themselves, "Let's see if this kid is really worth the hype." The pressure got more and more heightened. I tried to ignore it, but before every game I was nervous. However, as soon as I touched the ball, all the nerves went away. And besides, I knew in order to become an elite player, a professional, this was part of the deal. You became the dude with the X on his back. While you have people rooting for you, hoping you make it all the way, it's also expected that there will be others who are hoping that you fail so they can tell their boys, "Yeah, I saw Chris Jackson—he wasn't all that!" That way, they can feel better about themselves and have the spotlight turned in their direction.

As I pushed myself toward my NBA goal, a question sat on top of my head like a weight I couldn't lift: *How much will I grow?* This question was directly connected to another that had been torturing me since I was a little kid: *Who is my father?*

One day I couldn't stand it any longer. I felt like I had to know something. I went to my mom.

"Mom, okay. I know you don't want to tell me anything about my father, but is he tall?" I asked, holding my breath.

She looked at me in annoyance. "He's short!" she said.

She went back to what she was doing. Her two words cut through me like a machete. I ran into my room for some privacy, threw myself onto my bed, and wailed into the pillow. I cried and cried, sobbing for what might have been the end of my dreams, a lifetime of hard work being rendered almost meaningless in an instant. I was so devastated by what she told me. After the tears dried up, I started to get mad. I've always been that way — sorrow followed up by rage. I was mad at myself for indulging the self-pity, for letting myself entertain the thought that what she told me could curtail my dreams. I wanted to be great; I wanted to take care of my family, lift my people out of grinding poverty. I wanted to help others. I wanted to not be a failure. And deep down in my bones, I had always played with the thought that if I succeeded in basketball in a dramatic way, my father would step out of the shadows and introduce himself. He would be honored to finally claim me. I would be good enough for him to acknowledge that I was his. And I continued to push myself. Every jump shot, every drive to the basket, every free throw was fueled by a voice inside my head: *I'm going to show you.*

This information about my father wouldn't lessen my drive, I concluded. In fact, as I sat there on the bed, I pledged that I would work even harder, if that was even possible. After all, there were players who had played in the NBA who were under six feet. Calvin Murphy was one of the league's top scorers in the 1970s, and he was only 5'9".

I made a vow to myself: *Your dream is still possible.*

CHAPTER 7

Like many adolescent boys, I spent a lot of time thinking about girls. Looking at girls. Dreaming about girls. But not necessarily talking to girls. I mostly coveted girls from a distance. I was all about basketball, and I didn't want anything to block my path to the NBA. From everything I saw and heard, girls—and everything that came with girls—could turn my path in unfortunate directions. And I wouldn't be the first guy to be derailed.

Starting in elementary school, I had my share of interactions with girls. I went through the same stages as everybody else. Little crushes. A little bit of touching, feeling. Some kissing. But that was it. I was terrified of going any further than that. I just didn't want to get messed up.

In seventh grade, I was "dating" a girl named Denise. She was a ninth grader, two years ahead but in the same junior high. One day I told her that we could be girlfriend-boyfriend, but I also told her, point-blank, "Basketball comes first."

I think she was a bit surprised to hear me say that out loud, but she probably didn't take it too seriously. I think she might have chuckled a little when I said it. She soon found out exactly how serious I was. One afternoon when I went to the court after school, the ball just wasn't falling for me. My shot was off. Everything was rimming out, coming up short, going too long. I was "off." It happens to everybody, but I wasn't having it. I was devastated. I thought I knew what had happened: Denise. When I got home, I gave her a call.

"Hey, how you doin'?" I said when she answered the phone.

"I'm okay. How are you?" she said.

"Listen. I don't know what happened today," I said. "I don't know what's goin' on. I had a terrible day. My shot wasn't falling. I pretty much called to tell you I can't talk to you no more."

"Whaaat?!"

"Yeah. We have to end this," I said. "I apologize, but I got to figure this out." Then I hung up. It was over. I'm not even sure what Denise was thinking at that point.

The next day I was back on the court, working it out. And my shot was on fire. Everything was dropping. *Swish.* All net, all day. All the shots were working for me. I was feeling real good about my game, a radical about-face from the day before.

When I got home, I picked up the phone and called Denise.

"Hey, what's going on?" I said.

"Hey, how are you?" she said. Her voice was noticeably subdued.

"Listen, my shot felt good today. I was on fire," I said. "Couldn't seem to miss a shot."

She listened without saying anything.

"I was calling to see if you wanted to get back together?"

Long pause.

"Yeah," she said.

"Okay. Okay. We're back together then."

Sounds crazy, but that was me. The status of our "relationship" was determined by whether my shot was falling that day. Sex was all around me, seemingly everywhere I turned. And the thought of it excited me and scared me to death at the same time: What would happen if I did it and I liked it? What would happen to basketball, to my grand plans? No, I couldn't risk it.

I had a friend around this time whose name was Wayne. He was a smooth dude, very confident, comfortable in his own skin in a way most of the rest of us were not. We had a young, pretty Black teacher in the school all the guys lusted after, in the goofy way that boys lust after grown women. But Wayne didn't look at her like a little boy. Wayne talked to this teacher like a grown man. The way he complimented her, the way he would whisper something in her ear, it looked like a man coming on to a woman at the local bar. And most shocking of all, the teacher responded to it. When he spoke to her, I could see a change happen to her, right before my eyes. Like she was giving in! I couldn't believe what I was seeing.

One day, Wayne came up to me.

"Hey, Chris," he said, like he was about to share a secret. "I got that."

"Whaaat?"

"The teacher. I got that."

And I believed him. Wayne wasn't the type of dude to make stuff up so that he would look good. First of all, he didn't need to. He was good-looking, he was one of the best dancers around, and he was mature beyond his years. He didn't need to lie. I was certain he was telling the truth.

The thought of Wayne and the teacher stayed with me. Sex. Sex. Sex. I couldn't escape it. I could tell it was on the minds of the girls around me as well. One day when I was hanging out at the house of a girl in the neighborhood named Felicia, I found myself on the couch next to another girl, Michelle. Felicia's mama and her entire family were in the kitchen. I used to hang out there from time to time (I was friends with Felicia's brother), messing around on their piano, eating their food, spending time in their backyard. And they had a basketball rim. Always, basketball wasn't far from my mind.

Michelle and I were sitting on the couch, talking, when she made a move I didn't see coming. She threw a blanket over my head, climbed on me, and started trying to stick her tongue down my throat. With Felicia's mama and them in the next room. I was like,

What the hell, Michelle? I pushed her away. I didn't like her in that way, and I wasn't trying to get into something with all those grown-ups just feet away in the kitchen.

But all that activity certainly had an impact on me. Wayne and the teacher, Michelle and her probing tongue. I'd hear conversations in the neighborhood: so-and-so was having sex with his cousin, this dude was messing with that girl around the corner with the big boobs. And I was having my share of, um, nocturnal emissions during the night-time. I'd wake up to discover that at least a part of the dream I'd had actually did occur in real life, and the evidence was all over my sheets.

When I was in tenth grade, I started talking to a girl named Christy. She was a twelfth grader, the prom queen, and one of the most beautiful girls in the whole school, with a curvaceous body that looked more like that of a grown woman than a teenage girl. She was undoubtedly "fine as all get up," a phrase we used, meaning she was an attention grabber.

What I liked about Christy most of all, however, was not her looks or her body. What got me was her mind. She was the first girl I felt comfortable enough opening up to and being vulnerable about things I was seeing and feeling. And she understood me and would talk about her own stuff in a way that was unlike any conversation I had ever had before.

Man! I just love this girl's conversation! I would think after another long phone session. Clearly, things were progressing to the point where something was about to go down. And I was still terri-fied. I had heard so many stories about guys getting messed up when they got a girl pregnant. They'd have to go and get a job and put any dreams they had to the side. I was incredibly turned on by Christy, but I was afraid of something like that happening if we had sex.

From an early age, one of my motivations for making it out of the hood was to one day have a full-fledged family and provide my kids with all the things I never got. I don't know how many teenagers in their sophomore year of high school think like this, but even in elementary school that was always in the back of my mind. Basketball was my means to getting this family I dreamed about. Again, it all came back to basketball. Christy was making me think about how great it would be to have a girl like her by my side, a partner. I could imagine her one day being my wife. That thought motivated me.

Christy wasn't a virgin like I was. So I knew, once I decided I was ready, it was gonna go down. One night when we were riding around in her car, we decided to stop in a random parking lot. We were talking and looking at each other, the tension increasing by the minute. Finally, Christy climbed into the back seat.

"Come on back," she said in her intoxicating voice.

"Huh?" I said, trying to delay the inevitable, but sounding pretty dumb in the process.

"Come on to the back," she repeated.

I took a deep breath and joined her in the back seat. We went at each other, kissing and touching and stroking. *Uh-oh. This is it,* I thought. But the accompanying thought was: *Dang, I don't have a condom. I wonder if Christy does?*

For a dude who was so paranoid about getting a girl pregnant, you wouldn't be wrong for expecting that I would be a little better prepared. But I was young and dumb, and I was not a Boy Scout.

After a bit of foreplay, clothing started getting removed, and the next thing I knew, I was inside of Christy. But I have to confess that my heart wasn't into it. I was so distracted by the fact that I was in there uncovered that it was a seriously half-hearted encounter. Like, I was doing it, but I was not really doing it. All along, I'm thinking, *This is fornication — what if we get caught? What if she gets pregnant?*

My dreams of basketball will end. Am I satisfying her? Man, this feels so damn good. All these thoughts are moving through my mind like a movie montage.

The single-minded commitment just wasn't there. After a bit of thrusting, I pulled out. I didn't come inside of her. So at least there was that. After we got dressed and we were pulling out of the parking lot, my heart did several palpitations when I realized we had parked next to a church. Oh my God! Talk about your bad omens.

When I woke up the next morning, I felt a sense of relief and accomplishment for having crossed the barrier to "manhood." But all the while I was thinking that I needed to get to the courts. Once I got there with a ball in my hands, I went crazy. I trained harder than I had trained in years. I felt as if I had to go this hard to counter the yearning that was growing inside me, the strong urge for S-E-X. When I was inside Christy, I was dismayed by how good it felt. I understood how people could get so obsessed with sex that everything else just flies out the window.

If I was going to keep spending time with this girl and having sex, besides making sure I was protected, I needed to be certain that basketball was not going to suffer. So I had to go at it *hard*. I had to make sure I was taking care of business. If I didn't, I knew I would carry around such an overwhelming guilt that I'd have to chase her away. And I definitely didn't want to do that.

After that first time, every time I was with Christy, I was still hyper-paranoid about getting her pregnant. I had heard about condoms breaking, so I was constantly pulling out and checking on things, making sure it was still intact. Christy must have wondered what was wrong with me, but I couldn't help it. That was the only way I could feel comfortable enough to keep going. But it must have been okay because she never complained.

CHAPTER 8

It wasn't until ninth grade when my mother's curiosity about this basketball stuff finally moved her to come to one of my games. Up to that point she was mostly indifferent. That was her mindset: *Leave Chris to his ball, as long as he's doing what he's supposed to be doing at school and around the house.*

I was about to leave, saying to her, "Mom, I gotta go to my game."

She looked up. "Okay, well, I'm coming," she said.

"Huh?"

"I'm coming to the game," she said.

"Why are you going to the game?" I asked.

I was a bit surprised by how disturbed I was by her pronouncement. Since she had never been to one of my games, I had no idea how I would react. The crowd could get pretty intense, even nasty at times. I was worried that I'd be distracted if I knew my mother was in the stands, listening to what people on the other side might be yelling. I didn't want to be tempted to run into the stands to defend her honor or something crazy like that. I'm sure she was hearing about me from her friends and associates, telling her, "Jackie, you need to go see him play!"

"Aw, Mom, why don't you stay home?" I said. She glanced at me, probably wondering why I didn't want her there. She waved me away.

Despite my wishes, my mother came to the game. There wasn't any drama; I had an impressive game, scoring in big bunches. My mother had a great time. After the game, she said to me, simply, "I really enjoyed myself."

It wasn't her style to be gushing to me about how great I was. In fact, throughout my entire basketball career, even after I reached the highest levels, I don't think she ever gushed. Not even once. Just wasn't her style. But she did like watching me. Once she got a taste of it, she kept coming.

I got plenty of encouragement from my family, and there were also other adults who were supportive and important to my development off the basketball court. One of my teachers at Gulfport High, Miss Lindsay, was a steadying presence in my life. She was one of those tough teachers who didn't tolerate any foolishness. She could quiet a classroom with just a look, kind of like a surrogate mother standing in front of us. She sometimes joked with us, but even when she was joking you knew she was only half playing. Part of her was dead serious. I had a great deal of respect for her. I knew that when she was tough on me, when she was pushing me, she did it out of love. She clearly wanted the best for me. Excuses weren't going to work with Miss Lindsay. "I know you can do it!" she would say to me.

She knew what a young Black person would be facing outside of the school building. She acted like part of her job description was to prepare us for life as Black men and women in America. I looked forward to her class, even though I knew at any moment I might be squirming from her asking me tough questions or pushing me further than I wanted to go. Miss Lindsay was genuine.

Another influential teacher was Mrs. Miller, an English teacher. She was the wife of Eddie Miller, my AAU coach. Mrs. Miller was a slight, soft-spoken white woman who also clearly cared about me. She had extreme patience with me. I knew that she always had my best interests at heart.

School and I were never going to be best friends. I was a solid C student, doing just enough to get by, just enough to stay on the basketball court. I had no interest in being an honor roll student.

However, at the start of every school year, I would pledge that this time it was going to be different—I was going to buckle down and kick some butt in the classroom. I would be all excited and motivated, sitting there in the classroom with my fresh notebook and new pens and pencils. But the feeling wouldn't last. It would fade away, like the setting sun.

I think a big part of the problem was I never developed the discipline to be consistent, to sustain the concentration needed to be a good student. My environment didn't help, either. We didn't have books around the house; we weren't pushed to excel in school. I'd hear about families where the mom and dad made the kids read, made them do extracurricular homework, made them go to enrichment programs in the summer. That was not my house. Basically, all I heard was "If you got homework, do it. And don't come in here with no failing grade." But I wasn't restricted in my television viewing or anything like that. I'd come home and rush through my homework so I could move on to the stuff I enjoyed. I wasn't giving my work any more thought than was required to complete the assignment.

Even though I was in Mississippi, the state with perhaps the most notorious racial history in America, I didn't have much occasion to think about the destructive effects of racism in those early years. I was surrounded in the ghetto by poverty, by desperation. I was aware of how people on the other side of the tracks in Gulfport were living. The nice side. Basketball was taking me to a lot of places outside of my narrow little world. But still, poverty in my eyes was normalized. It was the way everybody I knew lived at the time. It was just the way things were. With normality comes acceptance.

It wasn't until I came across the television mini-series *Roots* when I was about eight years old that my eyes opened a bit. I started to think more deeply about the plight of Black people, how we were dragged over here and brutally mistreated for hundreds of years, and I began to get angry. I started to look at white people differently.

When I was younger, I regularly cut grass for a few white people in Gulfport to make money. One day while I was cutting for an older white lady, a lady who had always been very nice to me, I was a little disturbed when she kindly asked me if I wanted some lemonade. I thought back to *Roots*, to what happened to Kizzy. When she was a young girl, Kizzy played with the little white girl who was the daughter of her master. But when they got older, Kizzy was considered untouchable to the white girl. Kizzy had to stay away from her. When they were both wrinkled old ladies, the white girl drove up in her carriage and asked Kizzy to get her some water. The white woman didn't recognize Kizzy, but Kizzy surely recognized her. She pumped some water into a cup for the old white woman, but before she turned around, Kizzy hunched over and spit into the cup.

When the old white lady handed me the cup of lemonade, I stared down into it, thinking the whole time about what Kizzy did. Was it possible that this old white lady had spit into my lemonade?

I didn't take any chances. When the old lady went back inside, I poured that lemonade into the grass.

Unfortunately, I also began to develop a kind of fatalism about my life. From what I saw, good things just didn't happen to Black people. That idea stayed with me for a long time. It was fed by the shows I saw on television growing up: *Sanford and Son, Good Times,* shows like that. On *Sanford and Son,* they lived in a junkyard. On *Good Times,* they lived in the projects. Every time the show came on, we were all rooting for them to get out of the ghetto. And every time it looked like they were just about to make it out, something would happen to kick them right back in. Every time! That had a powerful effect on my young soul as I sat there watching this stuff. Every time they had hope, the life got punched out of them — and me. I'm seeing this, year in and year out. Negativity as powerful as radiation. Seeping into my brain. So when I began to achieve success on the basketball court, when I was breaking records and getting all kinds of accolades, I never could fully embrace the success. I was certain something bad was about to happen to me. That kind of negative energy just followed me wherever I went. In the back of my mind, I was always thinking that things could change for the worse at the drop of a hat. It was toxic stuff, sitting in my soul, pumping through my central nervous system.

I was increasingly aware that none of the systems around me seemed to be set up to enable Black people to succeed. I couldn't explain redlining or the inequities in the banking system, but I could tell that nobody seemed to care how we were living. I could see that the playing field was different. I could see that it was only white people living in the nice houses. It was only white people eating at the fancy restaurants. It was mainly white people traveling when I was in the airports. Clearly, this country had a vested interest in making sure that things stayed that way. These thoughts drove me to work even harder when I had a basketball in my hands. There was an air of desperation in the way I approached the game, like it was my only shot at survival. I wasn't playing.

Right before I went to junior high, I was walking on the beach near the public library when I saw a sight that stunned me. Marching on Highway 90, the shore road that went all the way west to New Orleans and eventually Houston, were about two dozen figures wearing crisp white robes that sparkled in the afternoon sun. The Ku Klux Klan. Parading in my city, right there next to the library and Central Junior High School. *Wow, I'm actually seeing this*, I thought. *Like, this is for real. Not some picture in a history book.*

There was no one around me, no commotion or protesters or spectators that I could see. Just two dozen dudes hiding their faces under white hoods. If they were covering their faces, that means they didn't want to be seen. Usually, you don't want to be seen because you're doing something you shouldn't be doing.

Why are they hiding? What are they afraid of? I wondered. *And how are they allowed to walk around like this?*

I don't remember feeling any fear. Mainly, what I felt was surprise. And perhaps a bit of confusion. Like, what was the point?

Later, when the idea of terrorist groups became a national obsession, my mind wandered back to that day at the beach in Gulfport. Forget about threats from foreign lands. The United States has been tolerating—and in many cases, supporting—a home-grown terrorist group for more than a century.

efore I even played a game of high school basketball, before I even put on my first Gulfport High School varsity basketball uniform, the Mississippi papers put me on the preseason All-State first team. That's how much anticipation — and pressure — greeted my arrival to high school basketball.

In fact, I started receiving recruitment letters from colleges before I even got to Gulfport High School. Louisville sent me the first letter when I was still in junior high. By the time I began practices at Gulfport High, things were getting pretty intense. I began to feel the weight on my shoulders, which just pushed me to work even harder. I wanted to validate all the preseason hype.

Coach Jenkins was tough to play for, but I learned an awful lot from him. His teams ran a flex offense, which involved a lot of running, picks, and screens in the half-court, with the ultimate goal of causing a defensive mix-up that would lead to an easy basket. Jenkins sent a steady stream of players on to get Division 1 scholarships, so I knew I was in good hands in moving toward my NBA goal. Coach was a World War II vet whose leg had been blown up in the war, so he walked with a peg leg. He had also been a prisoner of war in Germany. There was a lot of gravitas behind his words.

One of his trademarks was his incredible, meticulous organization. Coach Jenkins graded every practice, giving each player a numbered grade on everything from steals to points to charges. He decided who would start based on who had the highest total grade in practice. What that did was make the practices extremely competitive. If you had two or three guys with grades that were very close, and we had a game coming up, they'd be going real hard in practice — diving for balls, taking charges, going at each other. This happened every day, resulting in a tough, highly competitive team. He did the same thing with his AAU squad, so our lives year-round were ruled by these grades. He videotaped every practice as well (decades later he still has the tapes, as well as the paperwork listing the grades, in file cabinets at his house in Gulfport).

Another Jenkins method that ultimately became extremely beneficial to me was his rule on free throws. We always shot free throws before practice, and if you had a streak going you would keep shooting until you missed, even if practice had already started. When you missed, you would join practice. On numerous occasions, I had streaks that went on so long I'd miss the entire practice. At least three times I got more than 200 in a row; I've still got the practice free throw record at 286 in a row. The person passing the ball back after made shots and the shooter would together keep track; when you reached a certain number your name got put up on a board. There was the 25 club, the 50 club, the 100 club.

My free throw shooting elevated to another level during those years at Gulfport High. There are many aspects to successful free throw shooting — quality repetition, imagining hostile crowds, establishing a consistent rhythm — but a big part of it is about mind control: you must slow down the frenetic energy you normally have in a game and make your body and mind relax. This was essentially what I had to teach myself to do all day long because of Tourette; shooting free throws became second nature to me.

With such a system in place, it meant a lot to tell people you were a starter at Gulfport High School. By the time I got to high school, I had figured out how to work my intense, death-defying philosophy into the team game. I wasn't waking up at 5:00 A.M. anymore, but I was still pushing myself as hard as I could. I would keep going after practicing with the team, maybe working on a shot that wasn't falling the way I thought it should during practice. But often the coach would want us out of the gym, so I had to modify my obsessive compulsive disorder. I'd tell myself that I could leave after I made two or three shots that bounced off the glass in the exact spot I wanted or that made all net. After I got the two in a row, I'd throw the ball toward the rack or hand it to somebody so that I could leave the gym. The obsessive compulsive tendencies were still around, but I had learned how to better control them.

One day Coach Jenkins told me something that resonated with me so powerfully that it became a motto I have followed throughout my life. Coach, who knew I was a hard worker, came over to me after a particularly intense practice and said, "Give everything you have when you're training, because to waste one second, you can never go back and make up for it. It's gone."

Wow, that's true, I thought. *When you waste time, you really can't get it back.* In that moment, I pledged to myself that I wouldn't waste even the smallest amount of time, if I could help it. Working out hard, productively, focused on details, for one hour is better than working out two or three hours unproductively. Quality over quantity.

From the beginning, I was putting up big numbers at Gulfport High — if I might say, I was living up to people's expectations and shutting up the naysayers. I averaged about 21 points per game in my first season of varsity basketball. After the intensity of my workouts, game situations didn't feel overwhelming. High school defenses worked hard to stop me, but I trained to make things look effortless. I understood as early as elementary school that the easier you make it look, the more impressive it is. And if they did come out on me, I had no problem driving to the basket and getting my shots that way.

I was attracting tons of attention by my second year on varsity. Our games were packed. After a few games, crowds of little kids and grown-ups alike, even old men, swarmed around me and sometimes asked for my autograph. On more than a few occasions, security had to escort me to the bus because the crowds were so intense and chaotic. It was beautiful and crazy at the same time. I say crazy because one time a woman even grabbed my crotch. I slapped her hand down and went back to the locker room. I felt embarrassed and violated.

I also had something happen to me early on during that season that would profoundly impact me for the rest of my life. It happened after a game. Lillie Jenkins, the coach's wife—we called her "Miss Lil"—approached my mother. Miss Lil was a nurse by training, which perhaps explains why she felt compelled to ask my mother a question. I was close enough to hear the exchange.

"Miss Jackson, I'm not trying to overstep here, but I wanted to ask you something," she said. "We've been around your son Chris for several years now. We've noticed the tics and twitches. I would like to see if I can get him some help—if you give your permission."

My mother nodded. "Okay, no problem."

A few days later, Miss Lil took me to a building of doctors' offices about ten minutes from where we lived, next to Memorial Hospital. As I sat in the lobby next to Miss Lil, I could see a white guy who appeared to be a doctor walking by several times, watching me. Finally, Dr. Jackson called me back to his office. As soon as I sat down, he said, "So, you want to know what you have?"

I nodded. "I would like to."

"You have Tourette syndrome," he said.

No exams, no wires connected to my head, no EEGs. Just a few strolls through the lobby, watching me from afar. For the first time in my life, I had a diagnosis. It had a name.

"Tourette syndrome?" I pronounced slowly, trying out those words on my tongue.

He nodded, watching me for a reaction. He explained to me that Tourette is a neurological disorder that's hereditary, and it causes your mind to send mixed messages to your body.

He prescribed a drug called Haldol, which he said would help to control the tics. I started taking it daily, but I found out it didn't control the tics that much. I was still tic-tic-ticking away.

Worse, I soon discovered that Haldol had serious side effects. I was constantly hungry and thirsty. I was almost always sleepy. As long as I was moving, I was good. But when I wasn't moving, I was a zoned-out zombie. During practice, when the coach started lecturing us, I would constantly try to hide the fact that I was dozing off because I knew it annoyed him—as it should when it appears a person isn't listening. Because I wasn't concentrating on what he was saying, I wouldn't remember the instructions he just gave and would lean to a player real quick and ask what we were doing. Fortunately, most of the time I got the info I needed to do my job. If you're eating and drinking all the time and you're often sleepy, you're going to gain weight. I started senior year at 155 pounds; by the time the season was over, I was 170, even though I was playing games and practicing nearly every single day, constantly burning calories.

When I think back on those years, I have a hard time understanding why, with all the doctors, coaches, and teachers who probably watched me play from the stands, nobody ever asked me if I knew why my body moved like it did. But in their defense, they all probably figured that I knew about the Tourette, that my family had long ago dealt with it. As I did more research, I also saw that the condition often goes undiagnosed for a long time.

Those words from Dr. Jackson came like an early Christmas present. It was as if he had reached over and lifted a hundred-pound boulder from my shoulders. When you know something is wrong with you, but you have no explanation, no name, no diagnosis, it can torture you, make you wonder why you can't be like everybody else, make you pray to God for some sort of relief. Now I had an explanation of sorts. I was told that there wasn't a cure for Tourette, but it can be managed.

During my high school years, I made another connection with an adult that turned out to be meaningful. Her name was Miss January, and she was a middle-aged Black woman whom I befriended in tenth grade because she would come to the Gulfport High games to watch her nephew, Boo, who was one of my teammates. Though Boo was a year or two older than me, we had been playing ball together since we were little kids because he lived two streets over from me. Miss January, who attended all the home games with her sister (Boo's mom), took a liking to me. We just clicked. She became something of a surrogate mother to me, though at the time I wasn't thinking about anything like that. I just discovered that I liked talking to her. I could talk to her about pretty much anything—girls, sex, my future, the things that worried me, the things that angered me. Just about my life. We laughed together, got angry at similar things, and even cried together. She was a great listener; she made me feel totally comfortable. She was one of the coolest people I had ever met. I guess it was almost like an early form of therapy for me. She had two children, Crystal and Bo, who were still in elementary school, and a husband everybody called Jiggy. I became almost like a part of their family. One of my favorite dishes was her chili cheeseburgers; I would sit in her kitchen and have deep conversations with her while she prepared the burgers. To this day, I've never met anybody who could fix chili cheeseburgers like Miss January.

One day I got word through Miss January that I had been invited to an incredibly prestigious Nike basketball camp being held at Princeton University in New Jersey. But I never saw the letter from Nike, which I thought was weird. I had heard whispers about some of the more questionable aspects of Coach Jenkins's program. He was the winningest coach in the state of Mississippi and had done great things for basketball in the state, but there were rumors that he and his staff would hide many of the recruiting letters. I'm not even sure why. Maybe to increase the chances that students would stay in Mississippi to play basketball, or perhaps even to sabotage their opportunity to go further. Older folks would tell players to keep our eyes open, make sure we were aware of what's going on with our futures. Now I had some evidence that maybe this was true. The Nike camp apparently was inviting the 110 top high school players in the country. I was just a kid in Mississippi going out and playing ball; I didn't know anything about this separate solar system of prestigious camps. This was before the internet, so almost all of our knowledge of and contact with the outside world was in the hands of other people.

I knew I had to confront Coach Jenkins, but I was extremely nervous about doing that. Just like my family members, I was reluctant to confront authority. I suppose their behavior rubbed off on me. It was ingrained deep in the DNA of Black people in places like Mississippi, steeped in generations of racism and oppression. As a result, I had to be extremely upset to be pushed to stand up for myself, especially with white people. I became more aware of that fact about myself during my teenage years . . . and I didn't like it. When a situation called for me to push back against white authority, I would ask myself, *Why am I nervous?*

When I looked into my invitation to the Nike camp at Princeton, I also discovered that I had been invited to another camp in North Carolina, but it had already passed. I couldn't believe I had missed it. I was outraged. With the help of Miss January, I called the officials who ran the Nike camp.

"We sent it to you," the guy told me.

"I never got the letter," I said.

What happened to these letters? Who was standing in the way of my path to the NBA? And why?

As I headed to Coach Jenkins's office in the gym, I was filled with rage. I walked into his office wearing my game face, no smile, not the friendly, sometimes passive, let-things-slide person I often was. My future was on the line—a future that could possibly get me and my family out of the undesirable position we were in.

"Hey, Chris, what's on your mind?" the coach said with a cheerful, unsuspicious grin.

It wasn't my intention to be diplomatic or engage in small talk. I went straight for the jugular. "Listen. Information came my way that I was invited to a camp that I already missed. An invitation that was sent to you guys here at Gulfport High School. And now I'm invited to a camp in Princeton, New Jersey, the Nike camp. One hundred and ten of the top players are supposed to be there. Again, they said they sent me letters, but I haven't received them."

Coach Jenkins squirmed in his seat a bit. He didn't deny it, but instead said, "Well, I don't think you need those camps. You get as much publicity as you need here in Mississippi."

My eyes got real big. I couldn't believe the arrogance he was showing, to assume he knew in this case what was best for me—and without even informing me.

"Coach, there's no way in the world that I'm going to get as much or more publicity here in Mississippi than I'm gonna get at a Nike camp that has a hundred and ten of the top players in the nation. And colleges from all over the nation are going to be at that camp." I looked him in the eye.

"You don't have the right to hold this information from me." I paused. "I'm not here to seek your permission," I said. "I'm just here to tell you I'm going to the camp whether you like it or not!"

Coach stared at me for a few seconds without responding. "Okay, okay," he said with a sigh and a nod.

He knew he was wrong for what he did. There wasn't much he could say to me. I also found out that his assistant, Coach Austin, who coached the junior varsity team and who actually worked at the high school (Coach Jenkins was not a member of the faculty), was in on the deception because most, if not all, of the letters came to the school. So, he was the first one to see the letters. Over the years, I have sat and wondered about the thought and energy it takes to do what they did. What goes through a person's mind to contrive such a scheme to deprive people of all the choices they should have a right to consider? How could you comfortably live with yourself?

After the confrontation, my demeanor changed toward Coach Jenkins. He would try to make friendly small talk with me at the start of practice, but I wasn't interested. When he would make jokes, I wouldn't smile, I'd just stare at him. I couldn't get past what he had done. I kept wondering how many other people he had done this to, stifling careers. Here I was, busting my behind on a daily basis, all the while assuming I was in a partnership with the coaches, that they had my back, only to find out they were actively working against me. It just didn't make sense to me — after all, if I do well, the coaches would look good, right?

Eventually I softened up a bit. I concluded that I was going to be tied to this dude for the next year and a half. There was no point in making him into an enemy. I might as well let it go. He was trying real hard to make amends, to show me he was sorry. So, I let him back into my good graces. But I never forgot what he did. Also, to make sure it never happened again, I informed the women in the school office that from now on, they should forward all my letters to my house.

Letters from the most prestigious basketball programs in the country began to fill up the mailbox at home: Georgetown, North Carolina, Kentucky. I flew up to New Jersey for the Nike camp and pretty much had my way against the top talent in the country.

At one point, the high school recruiting publications like *Blue Ribbon College Basketball Yearbook* and *Street and Smith's* ranked me as the number one guard in the nation. I was told that a top scout at the Princeton camp, who had been going to the camp for many years and was considered one of the toughest scouts in the country, said he had never before given a player at the Nike camp a grade of 5. A 5 meant that in his eyes you were pretty close to basketball perfection. He gave me a 5 at the Nike camp in both the eleventh grade and the twelfth grade.

I'm a modest guy by nature. I never liked to pound my chest and draw attention to myself, particularly after the incident in my childhood when that older guy cursed me out. But I don't think I'm being immodest by saying I was killing it in high school. In fact, videos of some of my biggest games are still up on YouTube. In a tournament game in Lake Charles, Louisiana, against Washington-Marion High School, one of the top teams in Louisiana, I scored 55 points. In a winning effort, I might add. People were calling me one of the greatest high school basketball players in Mississippi history, words that just blew me away.

With the attention from colleges and scouts came sometimes weird attention from unusual places in Gulfport. Miss January told me that a man named Dr. Dunn wanted to meet me. While Dr. Dunn was well-to-do, he still lived in the hood, in the Quarters neighborhood where I had been born by the hands of a midwife. When I saw his house, it didn't stand out to me as something special. Of course, it was a lot bigger and nicer than ours, but nothing I thought complemented his professional title. He was a general practitioner, and his office was right next to the house, a small wooden building that was very modest. Miss January had told me that he was going to put me on an allowance: he would give me fifteen dollars a day to start with, just to make sure I had some money in my pocket. I was floored, and more than a bit suspicious. But she said he just wanted to support me and help me and my family make the best decisions for us.

Dr. Dunn was a light-skinned, heavyset, middle-aged man who didn't appear to be in the best health. He moved very slowly. When he turned around, he didn't turn his neck — he had to turn his entire body.

"Listen. First of all, I don't want anything from you," he said. "I just want the best for you and your mother." Over time, I came to discover that statement wasn't the full truth. But it sounded good at the moment.

After that meeting with him, Miss January became the liaison, passing messages from him to me. She told me he would get me a subscription to the local newspaper, the *Biloxi Sun Herald*. "He said every day this newspaper is going to come to your house," she said. "He doesn't want you reading sports. He wants you reading the other pages, so you can be aware of what's going on around you, what's going on in the world."

That turned out to be maybe the longest-lasting contribution he made to my development, putting me on the path to greater awareness, a path I would stay on for the rest of my life.

That fifteen dollars from Dr. Dunn, which usually got to me through Miss January, came in handy, allowing me to get extra food for lunch and grab snacks whenever my stomach was growling. In addition, every single morning Miss January would bring me a breakfast sandwich from McDonald's before I left the house to get on the bus. My mother was already gone to work; I'm not even sure she was ever aware of my morning breakfast delivery. I didn't have to worry about my stomach growling.

A few months later, I decided to test whether Dr. Dunn was serious when he said I could come to him if I needed anything. I was dating a girl named Patrice, and I wanted to treat her to a trip to New

Orleans, that gleaming, seductive, nonstop party town about ninety minutes west of Gulfport. I headed to Dr. Dunn's office. I wasn't comfortable asking anybody for money, but I was curious to see what he would say.

"Um, Doc, I'm trying to take my girl to New Orleans," I said, fidgeting a little in front of him. "Um, I'm trying to do this, you know, and you asked me to come to you."

Doc reached into his pocket and, like I had seen many old Black men do, pulled out a big wad of bills wrapped with a rubber band. He peeled off a small stack, hundreds and twenties. It was $600. To a high school student, that might as well have been $6,000. I'm sure my eyes got real big. On that afternoon, I found out Doc was not playing.

Over the course of the next nearly two years, I went to him maybe three more times for money for special occasions, like prom night. I didn't want to abuse his generosity. For the most part, the fifteen-dollar-a-day allowance, the daily newspaper, and the morning breakfast suited me just fine.

CHAPTER 10

Throughout 1987 and into 1988, my junior and senior years of high school, I had a steady stream of some of the most celebrated college coaches in America sitting in my living room or visiting me at school. Guys like John Thompson at Georgetown and the assistant coach to Dean Smith at North Carolina. After a while, though, I grew tired of all the courting. And the lying. I was grateful, flattered, but at some point, it became too overwhelming. I got to where I didn't even want them coming to talk to me. You know when you're shopping for cologne or perfume and you smell so many that you get confused and can't even tell which one you like? That was me with these coaches, who were all promising me a big future they couldn't guarantee. If I went to their school, they guaranteed that I would start right off the bat. As I sat there listening, I'd be thinking, *How can you guarantee that? You have no idea what will happen over the next year or two. How do you know? How do you know I'm gonna keep improving? You don't even know what's going to happen to us in the next thirty seconds! So how can you promise me? How do you know somebody else is not gonna come and outplay me?*

Because I was a Mississippi native, there was a great deal of interest in me picking a Mississippi school—as evidenced by the despicable actions of Coach Jenkins. I got a visit from Mississippi State, even though I didn't want them to come. But then I got a visit from Coach Dale Brown of Louisiana State University. He sounded totally different from the other coaches. When Coach Brown came into my home to recruit me, not once did he promise me a starting position. He told me they had a highly touted guard named Fess Irvin who was a freshman. Irvin had been a McDonald's All-American coming out of Louisiana. He told me that they would love if I came there and competed with him for the spot. It wasn't "You come, you start," like the others. I had a great deal of respect for Coach Brown for saying, "Hey, if you can play and you deserve to be out there, you'll play."

Man, that's all I wanted. Fairness. Just be fair. That speaks to the character of a person. And besides, how can you in good faith give me something I didn't earn, which means you deprived someone else of something they deserved? How can you then expect me to believe in the concepts of family and team when you give the hurrah speeches and not think this unhealthy favoritism can easily shift away from me? Once I got to their school, would all these other coaches make similar promises to the next hotshot guard who comes along the next year or the year after? The actions of the coaches brought me back to middle school, when my coach played the older guys just because they were older, not because they deserved it. I always had problems with that. That's not a good policy for the players who are receiving the preferential treatment and certainly not for the players who get the short end but deserve the starting nod. Whoever produces is who deserves to be out there.

On top of the words of Coach Brown, I was growing attached to Coach Carse, one of the assistants on Brown's staff. Carse, who is white, was someone I enjoyed talking to, and we almost *never* talked about basketball. I could talk to him about anything; I would tell him just about everything going on in my life during our nearly daily phone calls. We could joke with each other. I began to feel like he had my back.

I thought, *Either this is a hell of a recruiting strategy or this guy really does care about me, the person, more than basketball.*

During one of our conversations, I was moved to make a pronouncement.

"You know what, Coach? I'm not gonna go public yet, but I'm coming to LSU."

"Huh?" he said, clearly taken aback.

"You got my word. I'm coming to LSU."

Coach Carse was floored, since he, to his credit, had never overstressed the need for me to come to LSU. But people around me were advising me that I needed to say I was considering a Mississippi school, if just to keep folks in Mississippi from harassing me. That's why I always had Mississippi State on my list.

While I was performing at a high level on the basketball court, if I was going to play college ball, I had one enormous hurdle that I had to somehow negotiate: the ACT test. In order to qualify for NCAA competition, I needed a score of 15 on the test. I came along just two years after the NCAA instituted the requirement, called Proposition 48, which was vigorously attacked by the Black community because it was obvious from the start that Black athletes were going to be much more severely impacted. In 1986 and 1987, the first two years the new rule went into effect, the overwhelming majority of recruits who were ineligible because of the new mandate were Black.

I had gotten through my academic career up to that point by basically memorizing the things I needed to know to get a passing grade. Actually learning the material wasn't something I considered a priority. This was probably the worst imaginable preparation for a standardized test that's supposed to assess your cumulative knowledge. I could read a lot of words, spell a lot of words, but I had no idea what many of the words actually meant. If I came across a word I didn't know, I would just keep it moving. I wouldn't bother to take the time to go look it up. It was an intellectual laziness that still pains me when I think back on my mindset at the time.

In addition, there was always Tourette sitting there, messing with me. Taking a three- or four-hour test requires a great deal of concentration, discipline, and the ability to sit still. Each of those things was almost impossible for me to master. Once you sit down to take the ACT, you can't look around. You can't endlessly fidget. You can't get up and walk around. You can't waste time by staring out the window and daydreaming. You have to zoom in on the words on the page and stay there. That was stuff that had never been required of me during my years of schooling.

Despite all my challenges, the first time I took the ACT, I managed to come within a point of getting the score I needed to be eligible. I was encouraged by that; I knew eligibility was definitely within reach. At this point, Dr. Dunn stepped in. He paid for me to attend a test preparation course at St. John High School, a private Catholic school not far from Gulfport High, where they taught us tricks and tips to make the test easier. I took the test again after the course, but this time I actually went backward—I missed the needed score by three points.

Dr. Dunn made some more phone calls. He used my Tourette to get me special considerations. He arranged for me to take the test by myself at Gulfport High School with a monitor to oversee. I walked into the classroom that afternoon extremely nervous. I knew I had to get past this test if I was going to make my future happen. I couldn't even imagine what it would feel like if I didn't get the score I needed. What in the world would I do?

I was greeted by a nice Black woman, middle-aged and a little overweight. I've never talked about this before, but over the next few hours she proceeded to do something I know she was not supposed to do. At times she would hover over my shoulder, watching me fill in the little bubbles. Occasionally she would speak up.

"You sure that's the answer?" she would say.

I would erase the answer and pick something else. Then she would go about her business as if nothing had happened. She did this maybe about ten times. She never said, "Pick that answer," but she would nudge me in a different direction with her question. It didn't take me long to see the pattern that was developing. I'm sure there were answers I had wrong that she let go. We never had an actual conversation, though I'm pretty sure she knew who I was and what was at stake.

When I handed the test to her, I felt pretty good about my chances. I walked out of there a little more hopeful than I had been the other times, but by no means was I confident.

I had other adults who were popping up in my life at this time — in retrospect under somewhat mysterious circumstances. I was still a naive kid from the ghetto in Gulfport; I wasn't aware of the shady web of grown-ups looking to exploit an elite athlete who looked like he might be on the path to millions of dollars. I was eating in Sicily's Pizza one afternoon, taking advantage of the joint's all-you-can-eat policy. A young Black guy came up and introduced himself. His name was McNair. He said he had recently graduated from college and was about to become a chiropractor. He was friendly and seemed like a cool guy. After that, he would pop up unexpectedly in different places. I'd be working out on the playground basketball court and look up, and there he would be. During our conversations he told me he was about to open his own practice and buy a BMW, which was impressive to me, an impressionable teenager. We eventually became pretty good friends and would talk often on the phone. I hung out at his house sometimes, listening to music on his sophisticated sound system. After he bought the BMW, he let me borrow it to take a girl to dinner in Mobile, Alabama, during homecoming.

I was also befriended by another adult named Les Matthews, who took an interest in me and started showing up at places, acting like he was my friend. At the time, I had no reason to question my new friendship with either of these guys, since I thought both meetings happened by chance. But I soon found out that none of this was by chance.

I told Miss January that I had chosen LSU, and she quickly informed Dr. Dunn. She told me that he wanted to talk to me. In what seemed like an instant, Dr. Dunn showed up to my house in his big Lincoln. "Let's go for a ride," he said.

I climbed into the passenger seat. He directed the car onto the Gulfport slice of Interstate 10, the thoroughfare that stretches all the way across America from Tallahassee to Los Angeles, and then he said to me, "So where do you want to go?"

"I'm going to LSU," I said without hesitation.

He shook his head. "No, no, no. That's unacceptable!"

Wait, what?

"What do you mean?" I asked, glancing at him with a frown.

"We want the highest bidder," he said. "We want what's best for your family."

I'm sure my frown deepened. What in the world was he talking about, "the highest bidder"?

"UNLV offered a hundred thousand," he said. "UCLA offered a hundred thousand. We going for the highest bidder."

I admit that I was a little naive at the time, not being totally tuned in to the grimy underside of major college recruiting. But I had heard nothing about anybody offering cash for me to go to their school. I knew it was illegal to receive money under the table from colleges; I was scared to death of doing anything to endanger my college career. I should point out that I always believed the system as it exists exploits college athletes and makes millions on their backs without them getting much in return. I think college athletes should be paid. But I didn't want to get into any kind of trouble. I wanted to do things the right way.

I quickly grew outraged by what he was telling me. I tried to control it.

"Dr. Dunn, you told me yourself that you just wanted what's best for me and my family and that it's my decision to make. Nobody else's." I could see him getting angry. Then I added, "And besides, Miss January is cool with it also."

I thought about these dollars he claimed were being offered to my family.

"If I'm going to make it, if it's meant to be, my mother's going to be taken care of." I turned to him. "I'm not for sale," I said.

He looked at me with a scowl, but he didn't respond. The rest of the ride was quiet, as he fumed silently. But I was overwhelmed by what was happening. This was a person who was supposed to care about me. How could he be angry about me exercising my right to choose where I wanted to go? All along I thought he had my best interests at heart, and I was now discovering that Dr. Dunn was trying to sell me.

He pulled the car into the space next to my house. I walked into the house with Dr. Dunn following behind me. I was surprised to see Miss January sitting in the front room next to my mother. Waiting. *What is going on here?*

Dr. Dunn slowly trudged into the room, his health challenges evident with each heavy step. He was a well-respected, connected, and powerful man. And he wasn't happy. He eased himself down into the chair across from the couch where my mother and Miss January sat. I remained standing, hovering near the screen door. I wanted to keep my distance from this, whatever it was. I closely studied my mother and Miss January; they looked like misbehaving children who were about to be reprimanded by the principal. Or like southern Black people paying too much deference to white people, as I had seen my mother do on too many occasions.

"Miss January," Dr. Dunn said, directing his gaze at her, "did you tell Chris that no matter where he goes, you're happy for him — that it doesn't matter?"

Instead of answering, she dropped her head down to stare into her lap. I could not believe what I was seeing. Who was this person? I had spoken to this woman every day for months, revealing my hopes and dreams. She had always come across as a strong, independent woman. I didn't recognize this person cowering in front of this man. Was she just some sort of spy for Dr. Dunn all along?

They continued to talk. I heard things that shocked me. Dr. Dunn was in the process of building a condominium complex out near the airport, and he had promised my mother that if she cooperated with him, she would be placed in one of these brand-new units without paying a dime. My mother had been poor all her life; no one had ever promised her anything. This man was abusing her desperate need, manipulating and exploiting her for his own gain. Who knows if he was telling her the truth; he could just as quickly renege as soon as he got what he wanted, which apparently was for me to pick a school that would pay him money. I wasn't sure I should believe any of it.

After staring at them for several beats, I said to myself, *To hell with this!* I pushed open the screen door and aggressively walked away from the disturbing scene. It was the first time I ever walked out on my mother. I stumbled around the neighborhood in a daze, without a destination in mind. I was so full of anger and confusion I didn't know what to do with myself. I walked in the dark to the park on Second Street, one of my familiar basketball spots. These were the courts up the street from the Gulf, the most scenic courts in the area, where I used to do my early-morning workouts years ago. The courts were surrounded by lovely houses that always served as a reminder of where I ultimately wanted to end up. But I also knew I needed to play at the hood courts sometimes, to keep my edge.

I sat down on the steps of an old green house where the Boy Scouts usually met. I hung my head and finally let go of the emotions I had been holding inside. A flood of tears and rage flowed out. I cried like a baby, releasing the anger and disappointment, the sadness. And finally, the grief. As I cried, I cursed out loud, spewing words I rarely said.

"Fuck this, man!"

I had reached the pinnacle of high school basketball; all those years of grueling, grinding work were finally paying off. It should have been the happiest time of my life. Instead, it was the most miserable. I had been betrayed by people I thought loved me (however, I didn't include Miss January in that group). How would I ever get past that? How could I ever trust again? Love again?

I thought back on a curious scene with my mom that had occurred a few weeks back. I didn't understand it at the time; now it made a lot more sense. She had come into my room and sat down on the edge of the bed.

"Where you gonna go, Chris?"

I'd looked up at her. It was the first time she had come right out and asked me that question—the same one I had been getting everywhere I turned.

"Mama, I'm going to LSU," I said.

She paused. "I don't think that's a good idea," she said.

I frowned. "What do you mean?"

"Well, what about Georgetown?" she asked.

What did my mother know about Georgetown? I said as much. I suspected then that she had been talking to somebody. Now I knew that it was a lot deeper than that. She was a pawn in a larger scheme.

"No, I'm going to LSU," I said to her that night. "That's my decision. I have to be on that campus. I have to like the people that I'm with."

The last thing I wanted was to make a decision based on what somebody else wanted, even my mother. I was the one who had to live with it.

I wasn't sure if they were telling me the truth about schools offering money. I wasn't so naive that I'd never heard about athletes getting paid under the table. But I wasn't sure how Dr. Dunn had

become the person receiving the offers, if they did exist. Gulfport
was a small town; perhaps word had gotten out that Miss January
and Dr. Dunn were my mentors and benefactors. Colleges were used
to athletes having "handlers." Maybe somebody had told them that
Dr. Dunn was my guy. Who knows?

I eventually got up from the steps and walked to the house
of my friend Ronnie Harris, a teammate who lived nearby.

"I need a place to stay, man," I said. We went into his room
and I gave him the whole story.

"I walked out on my mom, man," I said. Then I started crying
again, right there in Ronnie's bedroom. "I'm just tired. I'm tired. I
just want to make my decision and keep it moving, you know?"

Ronnie nodded his head. He didn't have to say anything. I
just needed someone I trusted to whom I could unburden my soul.

Things remained tense between me and my mother. We were
conversing much less. I wasn't disrespectful, but I saw her differently
after that night. I was disappointed and disgusted, watching how
unassertive she was in not defending her son's right to choose—but
even more, in accepting the way Dr. Dunn addressed her, almost
like a child. I understood that she was poor and these people were
coming along and supposedly offering her riches. But I needed her to
understand that if we did this the right way, she would be more than
taken care of. She just needed to wait a few more years.

In the internet age, when rabid fans around the country can track
what elite players eat for breakfast, it might be hard to imagine that I
graduated from Gulfport High in 1988 without announcing where
I would attend college. Most scouting publications and experts were
calling me the top high school guard in America, yet I entered the
summer not having made a decision—at least not publicly. I was
trying to get through the pressure while dealing with the daily

drama that was playing out in my circle, created by the people who supposedly loved me.

My mother hadn't given up yet on trying to direct my decision. She even called up to Detroit to enlist the services of one of her brothers, my uncle Len.

Uncle Len was a scary dude, a bodybuilder who wore a permanent expression of displeasure on his face. You know how some people look mean even when they're in a good mood? That was Len. He was known as our family enforcer, the guy you'd call if you were in some sort of trouble and you needed somebody to come in and clean things up. He was a man's man. Len didn't appreciate hearing about anybody messing with his family. He took that very seriously. People in the family knew that you didn't call Len unless it was absolutely necessary, 'cause you couldn't be sure about what would happen when he arrived. Len was summoned when one of my aunts was being abused by her boyfriend. He hopped on a flight from Detroit and went looking for the dude as soon as he landed. He found him at some bar and literally beat him up and down the block, punching him, kicking him, throwing him into stuff—and talking to him the whole time.

"Don't you ever in your motherfuckin' life put your hands on my family!"

The beating quickly became neighborhood legend, a story that spread like a forest fire. That was my uncle Len.

I suppose my mother thought that Len would be able to talk some sense into her knucklehead son. But that's not how Len operated. He was going to get to the bottom of the situation before he decided how to respond. After he landed in Mississippi, he became my overseer for about a week, going with me to the courts and everywhere else I needed to go. I was happy to see him, but I wasn't happy about why he was there, which I assumed was to get me to change my mind about LSU.

He came with me one night when I went to the courts to shoot at about 2:00 A.M. It was something I did from time to time; I would drive my mother's car and keep the headlights on, directed at the courts, so that I could at least see a little bit. But I didn't mind shooting in the partial darkness because it improved my touch. If you're going full speed and can see only the outline of the rim when you're shooting, it will be easy in the light of day.

One day when we were walking back from the grocery store, Len finally asked me the question. He had been with me for at least a week and hadn't asked it.

"Where do you want to go?" he said.

"Uncle Len, I'm going to LSU," I said.

He stared at me without saying anything.

"You really want to go to LSU?"

I nodded. "That's where I'm going, Uncle Len."

"But what about—"

"Those other places are where *they* want me to go. But it's my decision. I'm the one who has to live with this decision. You know what I mean?"

He looked at me and nodded. "If that's where you want to go, then that's where you're going," he said.

We started walking.

"Listen. Right now, don't say anything to your mother," he said. He stopped and looked at me again. "I'm gonna tell you something. Once you make this decision, I'm warning you, you're going to have to be strong. Because your mother is going to make you feel guilty. She's gonna try to put a guilt trip on you. You're gonna have to fight through it." He nodded at me. The decision was final.

"Don't say anything now. But when it's time to go, you go."

I started telling him all the behind-the-scenes stuff I had been dealing with over the previous months, about all the people like Dr. Dunn and McNair the chiropractor and Les Matthews.

"My mother is getting this stuff from Dr. Dunn. I know it," I told him.

Uncle Len asked me a lot of questions about these adults who had inserted themselves into my life. I told him everything. One day when we were driving, I pointed to a condominium complex.

"That's where Les Matthews lives," I said.

Initially I had thought they were all people I had randomly met, but I was shocked to find out they all knew one another. They were some sort of team. Dr. Dunn had moved Les to Gulfport specifically to befriend me and stay as close to me as possible. Their plan was to become the team that managed my finances, endorsements, et cetera. When they looked at me, they saw dollar signs. I had been set up.

"Nephew, if anything happens to me before you get to LSU, give me your word that you're gonna go to LSU," Len said after we passed the complex.

I didn't like the sound of that statement. What was he going to do?

"Come on, Uncle Len, we don't have to talk like that," I said. "Let's just get to LSU."

But he repeated himself with a deadly stare. "If anything happens to me, go to LSU."

I nodded. "All right, all right."

When we got home a bit later, my mother ran out of the house with a big smile on her face. She was happy about something.

"Hey, Len!" she said. "Les wants to talk to you!"

Uncle Len now knew exactly who Les was. He gave my mother one of his withering glares. I could see her expression changing. Suddenly she wasn't quite so happy.

"He wants to come over and talk to you," she said. Her smile had faded. "He wants to come by," she repeated, sounding a bit uncertain.

"Yeah, you tell him to come on by. I want to talk to him," Len hissed.

My mother's eyes got real big. She turned around abruptly and started running back toward the house. I knew exactly what she was doing: she was going to call Les and warn him to stay far away.

When I got out of the car, Len told me, "Go get your stuff."

My mother turned back around. "What you talkin' about? Stuff for what?"

"Jack," he said, using the family's nickname for Jacqueline, my mother's name, "he's going to LSU."

My mother started shaking her head. "No! Len, you can't take my child! No, Len, you not doing this!"

Uncle Len ignored her. "Go get your stuff, Chris. Pack your stuff. Let's go."

"What are you talking about?! You ain't taking my son! Don't pack your stuff, Chris! Don't pack your stuff! Len! You can't!"

My little brother, Omar, who was twelve at the time, was sitting on the steps, taking it all in. His head was hanging, like he was about to cry. I was his protector, his big bro, and I was about to leave him behind. My heart ached for him. I had serious concerns about how my absence might affect him. The odds were that it wouldn't be good.

I went into the house and started packing. I could hear my mother still cursing Len out. But I knew it would have no effect on him.

After I stuffed a big bag with mostly shorts, T-shirts, and sweats, I went to put it in the car, the whole time telling myself not to look at Omar because I didn't want to cry. I climbed into the passenger seat and gave my mother one last look. Then I looked at Omar.

I gritted my teeth and turned away. As Len backed up the car and began to drive off, I couldn't hold it anymore. I let go of the anguish, the grief, the rage, allowing it to come out in a flood of tears.

"Get it out," Len said. "Get it out, nephew. It's gonna be all right. Just get it out."

As the tears subsided, I started getting mad at myself for crying. "Fuck!" I yelled out. "I'm gonna make it! Ain't no fuckin' choice! I'm gonna make it!"

Len nodded. I could see him smile. He knew it was true.

During the two-hour drive west to the LSU campus in Baton Rouge, my emotions seesawed between sorrow and anger. I knew I was about to take a huge step into the next chapter of my life, which brought me so much closer to making my NBA dream a reality. But I couldn't help but be sad about what I was leaving behind. Gulfport was the only home I knew. It had its challenges, but it had also been really good to me.

I could hardly contain my excitement when we hit LSU's beautiful campus. It was early summer, so the flowering grounds were still in their full glory. The timing couldn't have been better for me. I had turned nineteen on March 9, which meant that I didn't need my mother's permission to sign the LSU letter of intent. It was an occasion where my fourth grade stupidity, getting left back, worked out in my favor.

When we walked into Coach Brown's office, where I would sign my letter of intent, he greeted us with an extra-wide grin. He then blurted out, "Hot damn. The ship has sailed in! You passed the ACT by one point." Brown was already a big-name coach, widely celebrated for his skills at motivating players to achieve beyond expectations. LSU teams at the time had gone to the NCAA tournament nearly every year over the previous decade and had made the Final Four two times in the past eight years.

There were a couple of months yet before the semester would start. The coaching staff installed me in an apartment with two fellow incoming players, Vernel Singleton, a 6'7" forward also from Mississippi, and Stanley Roberts, a seven-footer from South Carolina. They both already had campus jobs and were settled in. I moved in with them, but I spent most of my time at the gym, getting ready.

I started my career at LSU with enormous hype, widely seen as the top guard in the nation. Though I tried to ward off the pressure, keep it at a distance, there were some questions bouncing around in my head. I had put up crazy numbers in high school, but what would it be like going up against the best players in the country? I had grown used to the burden of expectations, something I had been experiencing since elementary school. That burden made it so that I never felt like I could relax. Ever since that first game I ever played, when I scored 21, I'd never totally been at peace on the basketball court. I'd always felt that somebody out there was pushing himself to be better than me, so I couldn't let up. In the back of my mind, I always heard a voice: *They're gunning for you, Chris. You gotta be ready.*

Through well-publicized scandals and widespread accusations, many big-name schools around the country were assumed to engage in shady recruiting practices, such as paying players. Those rumors had become part of the public consciousness, shadowing players like myself throughout our careers. Lots of people joked to me about getting paid in college, and I couldn't help but wonder if I had missed out on some gravy train. Even when I got to the NBA, guys would joke that I probably took a pay cut to go pro. When I would insist that was far from the truth, they would act like I was lying.

"You were the number one point guard in the nation and you went there for free?" one guy said to me in amazement.

I wondered if I was the only one who missed out on getting paid as a college athlete. It wasn't the kind of thing guys would ever reveal to their teammates, so I had no real way of knowing if I had missed out during the recruiting process. If somebody had told me he got cash, while I was averaging 30 points a game and foraging for food some nights, I would have been hot.

I did get money from an LSU booster, but it was a one-time thing. I think it was around seven hundred dollars.

While my confidence on the court was strong, my feelings about my academic career at LSU were an entirely different story. I was extremely nervous about how people on campus were going to perceive me. I knew I had serious limitations in the classroom and that I had spent most of my academic life lollygagging, not applying myself as I should. I wasn't sure how much was going to be expected of me, whether teachers would take it easier on me because I was a big name. I was worried that I would quickly be revealed as an impostor, a kid who didn't even belong in an LSU classroom.

The racial element was there as well, being afraid that people would just look at the Black basketball player as a dumb jock, and I wouldn't have the tools to ward off such a perception. I knew I could never escape the racial component; it was always there, in the negative stereotypes about Black students in school, especially Black male athletes. All the controversies about the NCAA's Prop 16, adopted in 1992, didn't help matters; they just brought more scrutiny to the reality that too many Black athletes hadn't been properly prepared to do college-level work.

In addition, there was Tourette. I had a whole new campus of folks who didn't know me, didn't know about my tics and twitching. What would they think of me when they found out, when they observed me? Would they accept me or think something was wrong with me? What would the girls on campus think?

By that time, I had learned how to camouflage a lot of my TS idiosyncrasies. But it's a delicate dance. If you're in the midst of doing something intense, if your heart rate starts going up, if you get real nervous, if you get angry — that's oftentimes when the Tourette will come out more visibly. I didn't worry about it around friends and family and people with whom I was comfortable. But with people I didn't know, I was always calibrating. I would care about what they thought of me and would be intent on making them feel comfortable and not be a distraction. But I knew that when I held it in, it would come out even worse when I was no longer in their presence. I'd get to the car or get back home, and it would explode because of the effort of holding it in check. Because of that, I began to feel that holding it in was one of the worst things I could do. To put people at ease, I learned to make jokes about myself to disarm them.

"You may see me over here moving around," I'd say. "Listen, I have Tourette syndrome and sometimes it gets on my nerves. It wants to do what it wants to do. I'm not crazy. I ain't gonna kill you. I ain't on that level, but me and the TS are constantly fighting each other over here."

Usually this resulted in a laugh. I'd laugh at myself sometimes. I knew that all the unusual movements might lead people to conclude that I might be a danger to them: "Is this guy going to pull out a knife or a gun?"

Eventually, people who were used to being around me would get to a point where they didn't even see it.

I spent just two years at LSU, and, for most of my time there, if I wasn't in class, I was in the gym or somewhere getting something to eat.

The competition in college was definitely at a higher level than high school; I'm not suggesting otherwise. But I found that the game still felt easy to me. I was shocked when the season started that I was able to get my shots off with no more difficulty than I had in high school and junior high. I was getting to the spots I liked without much interference. There were tougher teams that we faced during the season at Gulfport High, teams with big, strong guys who would force me to make some adjustments, maybe pick up my speed a bit or find ways to lull them to sleep before I exploded. So, I was used to making alterations to my game based on the level and type of competition I was facing. The same moves I had been doing for years — moves I had perfected from hours and hours of repetition during my personal workouts — were still effective at the college level. It was a great lesson to me on the importance of intentional, detailed, consistent hard work; I saw how much it truly paid off on NCAA basketball courts.

I did an interview with Kent Lowe, who worked in the sports media department for LSU, before the start of the season, and he asked me what I wanted to accomplish during my career at LSU. I told him if I could average 12 or 13 points a game with 7 assists, I would consider that a pretty decent career. I wasn't being overly modest; at the time, I meant it. And if I had said something like I wanted to dominate college basketball, it would have sounded crazy anyway.

Dominating was my goal, but you can't always express your aspirations to people, for multiple reasons: they may think you are foolish to have such a goal, they may think you are arrogant and selfish, and they may also try to dissuade you from thinking too big. I was 5'11½", maybe 6' with sneakers on, going up against a sea of towering players, many more than I encountered in high school, so I could be excused for being conservative in my predictions for what would happen.

In my first game, against Marist, I had a respectable 13 points in a win for LSU, a good start to the season. In our second game, we lost to Oral Roberts by 4 points, 100–96, and I finished with 25. As we filed off the floor at the end of that game, a disappointed team, Coach Brown stopped me before I stepped into the locker room. He put his hands on my shoulders and looked me in the eye.

"Chris, listen," he said. "We're going to need you to score more." I nodded. "Okay, Coach," I said softly. "I'll try." The memory is still incredibly vivid for me, more than thirty years later.

I went out and scored 48 in the next game, against Louisiana Tech. People were amazed that I was continuing my high school pace without a hiccup. After putting up 23 against McNeese State, we had Florida in our fifth game, which was nationally televised — the first time I'd be performing in front of a national audience in college. It's amusing to me to watch a video of the game on YouTube and hear the announcers reacting to my game. When I got to 42 points on a turnaround jumper from just inside the three-point line — at a crucial time, giving us a 5-point lead when Florida was threatening to tie the game — the television analyst Billy Packer exclaimed, "Awww, would you give me a break!"

A minute later, when I got to 45 on a leaner in the lane, plus a free throw, Packer said, "He is absolutely one of the premier point guards—"

"Already!" his cohost interrupted.

I even flushed a dunk on an alley-oop off a pass from the wing on a designed play that they never expected: I went around a screen, caught the ball at the height of my leap, and threw it down with two hands.

The Florida win happened to be Coach Brown's three hundredth at LSU, in his seventeenth season. I had no idea that I had scored so many points. I was back in the locker room — it was an away game in Gainesville — when Coach Carse ran in and started shaking me.

"They want to see you outside!" he yelled. "You gotta go do this — you just scored fifty-three points!"

"What?" I was taken aback. I had just scored 48 four days earlier. At the time, Florida was considered the top team in the Southeastern Conference, boasting a laundry list of former

McDonald's All-Americans. And we had played them in their place. *Wow, 53?* I thought. *Are you kidding?*

When I emerged from the tunnel and came back on the floor, the fans erupted in applause. These were Florida fans, showing their appreciation for my performance. *This is crazy,* I thought.

There were what seemed like a hundred journalists waiting to interview me at the postgame press conference. As I was answering their questions, I started to become alarmed. I thought back to my childhood, to those TV shows with the Black folks stuck in the ghetto. Here I am, sitting on top of the world. Is this gonna last? During the course of the questioning, my emotions jumped back and forth between being happy and being terrified. *Man, something bad is about to happen to me. I'm gonna get hit by a car. The airplane is gonna crash. Something.* As I sat on the bus headed for the airport, I looked out the window with fear in my gut. *This is too good to be true. It's gonna end bad for me.*

When we boarded the plane, I could feel the panic. As luck would have it, the flight was extremely bumpy for most of the trip back to Baton Rouge. We were flying through a bad storm and the turbulence was crazy. At one point the plane was dipping and jolting up and down so hard that I could see the wings flapping. When the plane started to move sideways, I just about lost it. *Oh God, I knew it!* I thought. *This was all too good to be true!*

Some of my teammates, however, were acting like we were on a roller coaster ride or something, all fun and games. That alarmed me even more. Maybe those guys just didn't think about death the way I did. It was something that was on my mind every day, not necessarily in a morbid way, but in a way that I felt brought me closer to God and made me more appreciative of my time on Earth, reminding me to at least try to maximize every minute of every day before it's too late.

The plane bounced around and my teammates hollered, "Whoooo!" like they were at Disneyland. I couldn't take it anymore.

"Man, shut up!" I said to them. "This ain't nothing to play with!"

They stared at me and quieted down a bit. I sat in my seat in disbelief, amazed that I had just conjured this scenario up on the bus and it was now seemingly coming true. I could see flashes of lightning outside the plane and hear the thunder rumbling. It was maximum drama in the air, and I was terrified. I had my eyes squeezed shut as I prayed as hard as I could, asking God to put us safely back on the ground.

When the plane finally landed, I was figuring out the words I would use to tell Coach Brown I couldn't do it anymore: "Coach, you know I love playing basketball. I do want to make it to the NBA. But I just don't want to fly anymore. I'm wondering if I can just play home games."

As we disembarked, I had second thoughts. *Man, if something's gonna happen to you, it's gonna happen. You need to suck it up, Chris! You can't go and tell that man you can't fly anymore. What are you thinking?*

I never said anything to the coach. But I didn't stop thinking about that flight, about how scared I was. However, I wasn't scared enough to stop working or pushing myself to the NBA, where I knew plane flights would be frequent.

We had several big wins that season that were considered upsets at the time. Probably the biggest win was when we beat Georgetown at the end of January. We played the game in New Orleans at the Superdome, and the crowd was enormous. There were more than fifty-six thousand screaming fans watching us play that day, reportedly the largest crowd ever to watch a college basketball game up to that point. John Thompson stalked the sidelines. He had tried to recruit me; I had a great deal of respect for him even though

I had no interest in playing for Georgetown. The game, which was
nationally televised, had gotten a bunch of hype. We were about
halfway through the season, and Georgetown was ranked number
two in the country. We weren't in the top twenty at the time, but
I think part of the reason we were getting a lot of attention was
because of my high scoring. The Georgetown squad was loaded with
future NBA players: Alonzo Mourning, Dikembe Mutombo, Charles
Smith, Jaren Jackson. Alonzo and Dikembe became superstars in the
NBA and eventually were inducted into the Hall of Fame. In other
words, nobody expected us to beat them. But as a team we embraced
the role of underdog. It gave us a huge dose of motivation, felling
giants — literally, in the case of Georgetown's twin towers, Mourning
and Mutombo.

The atmosphere in the Superdome was electric throughout
the game as we continued to trade baskets back and forth. At one
point in the second half, we built up a 10-point lead. But Georgetown
came storming back, led by their sharpshooting guard Charles Smith.
We prevailed, 82–80, when Ricky Blanton grabbed an offensive
rebound off a missed shot and put it in the basket at the buzzer. It
was such a big upset, we ran on the court and celebrated like we had
just won the NCAA tournament. After that win, we entered the top
twenty, ranked nineteenth in the country.

During the game, Billy Packer said something that upset a
lot of Black folks, particularly those back in Mississippi. After I had
made an impressive move, attacking full speed while changing direction and putting the ball between my legs without skipping a beat
or decreasing my speed, Packer exclaimed, "One of the things you
wonder about: How can a kid [from] Mississippi develop all of these
offensive fundamentals he's got?"

It was a silly, ridiculous comment, feeding into the stereotypes about Mississippi as an entire state of uneducated backwoods

hillbillies. Anybody who watched five minutes of a Gulfport High School practice with Coach Jenkins at the helm would have been eager to have him instruct kids across America on what strong offensive fundamentals look like. But here was Packer, assuming that a Bert Jenkins and other talented, creative young Black men weren't possible in Mississippi. If you sat back and thought about it just a little, you could conclude that growing up in the environments we did encouraged creativity just to survive.

I finished the game with 26 points. I was the high scorer for LSU, but I was outscored by Smith, who had 32 for Georgetown. I knew Georgetown would spend considerable energy trying to shut me down in the game, since I had been putting up such big numbers. But I had already gotten pretty adept at adjusting my game depending on what the defense was giving me.

Some guys are pure shooters, other guys are scorers. Some people can do both. I feel like I fall into the last category — I get mine through a variety of ways. I can get my shot off the dribble; I can come off screens; I can run the floor and catch and shoot. I learned how to watch my defenders closely, to see how they would react in various situations. I saw that if you're coming at a guy hard all the time, automatically he's going to be highly engaged. You've alerted him to have his antenna up at all times.

Therefore, many times I would come down and look real relaxed. Calm. I'd pass the ball, cut, go get it, put it through my legs, pass, cut again. I'd try to put the defender to sleep. When he'd been lulled, every now and then, while still in my slow motion, I'd pull up and BOOM!

The next time down, I might pull up right away and BOOM! Once in a while I'd explode and go hard. But then I'd go back to being relaxed, calm. It's about constantly changing speeds, changing angles, changing patterns.

After that big Georgetown game, we blew out Ole Miss at home, but then lost to Mississippi State at their home gym in Starkville. While the Mississippi games were a big deal to me for obvious reasons, I learned early on that it ate up Coach Brown to lose to a Mississippi school. Coach *hated* Mississippi. There's racism everywhere, but he considered the racism in Mississippi to be on another level. If racism were an NBA season, everybody else's racism was the regular season—well, maybe some states were the playoffs—while Mississippi's was the NBA Finals. Over his seventeen years of coaching LSU up to that point, Coach Brown had seen his Black players subjected to all types of hateful ridiculousness—the overt stuff, like guys being called "boy" to their face. I've spoken about the things I was exposed to at an early age, watching how the Black folks around me respond to whites, so nothing about Mississippi came as a surprise to me.

But Coach Brown was born and raised in North Dakota; he went to college and then started his coaching career there, remaining in the state until he was in his thirties. He moved around the country for coaching jobs, to places like Berkeley, California; Logan, Utah; and Pullman, Washington. So, he wouldn't have had much occasion to see up close the particularly potent racism of the Deep South. He took over as LSU head coach in 1972, replacing the LSU legend Press Maravich. I mean, 1972 was just four years after the assassination of Dr. King. Since then, Coach Brown had witnessed a whole lot of painful scenes.

Coach didn't even want us to spend the night in Mississippi, no matter how late the game was. We'd stay overnight in places like Alabama, Tennessee, and Georgia. Surely these places had their large share of racism, and of course we lived in Louisiana. But Coach Brown felt like Mississippi was different. He wanted to spend the least amount of money and least amount of time there. Instead of spending the night in a motel, right after the game we'd hop on the bus and leave Mississippi in the rearview mirror.

My games in Mississippi always had an edge to them because people were still mad that I had left the state. When I stepped on the court, I would be greeted by a chorus of boos. I still was nursing a serious grudge about the way Mississippi treated high school athletes.

The state had a rule that when athletes went to places like the Nike camp I attended in Princeton, not only was it against the rules for somebody else to pay my way, but I couldn't bring home any paraphernalia I got from the camp or I'd be endangering my high school eligibility. I thought the rule was outrageous, a way to punish poor Black athletes.

If I knew the word *oppressive* when I was a student at Gulfport High, I would have called it so. In order for me to attend the Nike camp, Dr. Dunn had to deposit money into my mother's account so it looked like she was paying my way. And they gave us a ton of Nike gear in Princeton, none of which I could keep. Imagine how that felt to a teenager, having to give away a load of expensive gear that I technically paid for by registering for the camp.

So, yeah, I had a major problem with the state of Mississippi. I can't help where I was born. While I developed many positive traits while I was in Mississippi, there were things about what Mississippi did to me that I never got over. What would have happened if I didn't have a guy like Dr. Dunn to foot the bill for the Nike camp? I never would have had the opportunity to play one-on-one against Michael Jordan, which I did at the camp.

After Shaquille O'Neal got to LSU the next year, we heard all kinds of nastiness from the stands when we emerged from the locker room at C. M. "Tad" Smith Coliseum in Oxford, Mississippi. Hell, the stadium was located on Confederate Drive.

"Go back to Africa, boy!" was a precious line I heard coming from the crowd, directed at Shaq.

Are you serious? I said to myself.

I turned to Shaquille. "Don't even worry about it," I said. "Let's get 'em, right here. That's the best thing we can do."

My philosophy was not only to always let them know that I was there but to leave a legacy: You will remember you couldn't do anything to stop me. No matter what happened in the game, whether we won or lost. If we happened to lose, I wanted the world to say, "Yeah, they lost, but that mutha gave y'all the business!"

After we lost to Mississippi State in Starkville in the beginning of February, we went on a little winning streak, beating Auburn, Tennessee, and Kentucky. I was putting up big numbers in each game. I scored 50 against Tennessee. After shooting poorly in the first half against Kentucky, I heated up in the second half and scored our last 16 points in a row, finishing with 26. Then we somehow got blown out by Vanderbilt in Nashville before rebounding to beat Georgia at home in Baton Rouge.

Right before we were about to play a big game against eighteenth-ranked UNLV—a squad that included Stacey Augmon, David Butler, Greg Anthony, and Anderson Hunt (Larry Johnson, the unstoppable power forward, wouldn't join the team until the following season)—I appeared on the cover of *Sports Illustrated* (February 1989).

On the cover, I am standing on an outdoor court at a playground about ten minutes outside of the LSU campus at sunset, holding a basketball on my hip and wearing purple LSU sweats with a yellow LSU T-shirt. The headline read "He's a Pistol." The subhead read "LSU Super Frosh Chris Jackson Evokes Memories of Pete Maravich."

In addition to talking about my skills and comparing me with

Pete Maravich, the article, by the writer Curry Kirkpatrick, went into my estranged relationship with my mom, stating that rumors were swirling that while I was being recruited, she had tried to sell me to the highest bidder and had refused to sign my LSU letter of intent. I made sure the article included that I had gone back to Gulfport after I got to LSU and had made up with my mom—and that she attends all our home games.

I was surprised and not entirely pleased by how much the article talked about Tourette:

What Jackson must still cope with is the perplexing disorder afflict ing his nervous system. Some of the symptoms of Tourette syndrome first appeared when he was in grade school, but he wasn't put on medication until the fall of 1987, when Jenkins and his wife became involved.

Blanton, whose locker is next to Jackson's, says that he has often been slapped by CJ's hand. And Jackson's knuckles have taken a beating from the involuntary pounding of his hand into his dormitory wall. "When I first came here, I knew guys were looking at me like, wow, this boy is crazy," says Jackson. "But, hey, this is just me."

I was freezing when I posed for the picture that went on the cover. I didn't own a whole lot of winter clothes, and LSU didn't pro-vide us with a lot of gear. I actually borrowed the LSU sweats from Coach Carse because I didn't have mine with me. I was filling up are-nas and appearing on the cover of an iconic magazine, but I was still a poor kid from Gulfport. That's the painful reality of major college sports. Everybody profits from a big star except the star. There's a picture of me in the article walking on campus, and I'm wearing tight black jeans and a light Sixers pullover. It was one of the outfits that I wore all the time; I had a few that I alternated.

After eating in the dining hall early in the evening, there were nights when I would be so hungry, my stomach would growl just like it did when I was growing up in Gulfport. I usually didn't have enough money to go somewhere and buy pizza or burgers like most of my classmates, feeding that late-night hunger that seems to be a perpetual feature of college life. There were nights when I called Coach Carse to tell him I was hungry.

"Look, Coach, man, I'm hungry!" I told him more than once.

He would bring me a couple of burgers from Rally's, a burger joint right off campus. The mind-boggling thing is that he wasn't supposed to do even that; it was against NCAA rules. The NCAA would rather have a coach ignore pleas of hunger from one of his players, if you can believe that.

We beat UNLV on a clutch three-pointer by Ricky Blanton at the buzzer. I had 29 points, including a two-handed dunk on a break-away. After the UNLV upset, we lost to Florida and Mississippi, and then Tennessee in the SEC tournament — all teams we had beaten during the season fairly easily. But the Mississippi game got a lot of attention because of what Gerald Glass and I did. Glass got 53 points, and I went for 55. Going into the game, our last regular season game, I was the top scorer in the SEC and second in the nation behind the incredible Hank Gathers of Loyola Marymount. Glass and I traded baskets for the entire game; it was almost as if we were playing a game of one-on-one, though the muscular Glass was a lot bigger than me at 6'5", so I wasn't usually guarding him. Although I missed a three-pointer at the buzzer and we lost, 113–112, I did hit two big milestones that night: I scored the most points in NCAA history by a freshman in a season, and the 55 points was the highest point total in a game by a freshman in NCAA history.

"I realized that all four NCAA scoring records are held by LSU players," Coach Brown said recently in an interview. "The sophomore, junior, and senior scoring records by Pete Maravich, and the freshman record by Chris Jackson. Chris actually could have averaged more than 30.2 points. I never told him not to pass, but there were times when he passed the ball and I wished he didn't. And he was such a tremendous free throw shooter — even if he couldn't get his shot off, when he went to the line he was shooting 90 percent."

Despite ending the year on a three-game losing streak, we did get an NCAA tournament invitation. We opened against University of Texas–El Paso, led by two future NBA stars, guard Tim Hardaway and forward Antonio Davis. The game was played on the campus of the University of Arizona in Tucson. It was an intense game. They were very good, better than us, with more weapons than we had. Hardaway and I didn't guard each other much, though the game was hyped as a matchup between the two of us. Tim was a real smooth, well-balanced player, not terribly fast but fluid, with occasional explosive bursts to get his shot off. His approach was to not push too much, to let the game come to him. And he was solidly built, very strong.

We lost by 11, 85–74, to get knocked out of March Madness. I finished with 33 points in the losing effort, while Tim put up 31. We were disappointed, of course, but if you play enough basketball you learn to take the bad with the good. We walked away knowing the things we needed to work on to get better and stronger. I had learned not to get too excited about the big games. I needed to stay grounded, to keep things on an even keel to play my best. If you get too hyped, your emotions can overtake you and hurt your game. Too relaxed isn't good, either. You gotta stay somewhere in the middle.

At the end of the season I won a ton of individual awards, most notably, SEC Player of the Year and first team All-American. All the other guys on the All-American first team were seniors: Sean Elliott of Arizona, Pervis Ellison of Louisville, Danny Ferry of Duke, and Stacey King of Oklahoma. My teammate Ricky Blanton was selected as an All-American honorable mention. I finished with a scoring average of 30.2 points per game, which was an NCAA record for a freshman. There was talk that perhaps I should come out and declare for the NBA draft already — Red Auerbach reportedly said I would be the first player chosen, or at least I would have been the Celtics' first pick. But I wasn't quite ready yet to make the jump.

CHAPTER 12

We started hearing about Shaquille O'Neal toward the end of the school year. We got a chance to watch him in action after our season was over, during the McDonald's All-American game in April 1989, showcasing the nation's top high school stars. I had just played in the game the year before with players like Alonzo Mourning, Billy Owens, Shawn Kemp, and Todd Day. We knew Shaq had already committed to LSU, so we were eager to check him out. A bunch of us gathered in Stanley Roberts's dorm room, right across the hall from mine, to watch the game.

We were quite impressed with Shaq's skills. Man, he had some bounce, he had some shake and bake. Early in the game, Shaq blocked a shot, grabbed the ball, and dribbled coast to coast, slamming it down at the other end — and taking off in the lane quite far from the basket, I might add. It was a crazy illustration of his skills. Guys in the dorm room lost it.

"Ooooh! Did you see that?! And he's coming here!"

Appropriately, just as guys were hooting and pointing, the famed commentator Dick Vitale excitedly said on the telecast, "They're gonna celebrate in Baton Rouge, Louisiana!"

But I could see the effect that his teammates' reaction was having on Stanley. The seven-footer had come in with me but couldn't play freshman year because of Proposition 48. Now he was watching his teammates get all animated, and I could see the pained expression on his face, as if he were thinking, *Man, I thought we were boys — were y'all this excited when you saw me play?*

Stanley would be directly impacted by Shaq's arrival. Stanley wasn't the hardest, most disciplined worker — a statement I'm sure he would agree with at the time. Shaq was going to push Stanley real hard to show a stronger work ethic if Stan was serious about leaving his stamp as a dominant player at LSU. Up to that point, Stanley had gotten away with leaning too much on his size and athleticism and not necessarily putting in the work. But as he watched Shaq that day, he knew deep inside that would have to change.

I went over to Stanley. "Hey, big fella," I said. "We know what you can do."

Elite athletes have a great deal of pride, so I knew I couldn't go too far in what I said to him. But I wanted to let him know that we had confidence in him, no matter how much hype was swirling around Shaquille O'Neal.

People in Baton Rouge were definitely excited about the arrival of big Shaq. At the same time, guys did have some concerns about what his presence might do to our team chemistry. These were the kinds of questions you would naturally have when a major piece was being added to the puzzle; they weren't so much specific to Shaq. *Is he going to improve the team chemistry or mess it up? Is he a good dude, or is he a knucklehead?*

One of the main things that worried me and others in the program about Shaq was his stepfather. Phillip Harrison, a career army sergeant whom everybody called "Sarge," was a nice guy, but he could also seem intimidating and aggressive to some. He was strong-willed and wasn't afraid to speak his mind. When he came around, the air changed in the building. It was understandable that he was just looking out for his stepson, but at some point you've got to let the coaches do their job. We all got the impression he was in Coach Brown's ear, trying to micromanage things. I felt like we didn't need that kind of energy around the team.

But once Shaq became one of the guys, he quickly dispelled any of those concerns. He was a good listener, he worked hard, and, best of all, he was funny. However, once the season started, Shaq and I did have some conflict. We actually had an altercation during a game. I came down with the ball, and Shaq felt like he was open under the basket and I intentionally didn't pass to him. He barked at me on the way back up the floor. I said something back to him. I can't remember the exact words that were spoken. I don't care who you are, how big you are, even if you're president of the United States, there's a level of respect I demand—because I'm the first one to give it.

Coach Brown noticed the altercation. The next day, Coach called both of us into his office. He told us to sit down.

"Tell me—what's the problem?" he asked.

Shaq went first and told the coach that he believed he should have gotten the ball because he was open. When he was done, I said, "Look, Coach, I understand the heat of the moment and all that, but there's a way you got to come at me. I don't respond kindly to people thinking that they can punk me, okay?"

I said that purposely not passing the ball to someone was not in my character—unless maybe I thought he needed to be taught a lesson. "You respect me, and I'll respect you," I said. "I'll even try to bend over backward for you."

Coach Brown looked back and forth, then he stopped at Shaq. He pointed to me and said, "You see this guy here? This is his team. If you want it, get it off the glass."

Things seemed okay between us after that meeting. We didn't run in the same cliques, so it wasn't like we were hanging together. I spent most of my time with Stanley Roberts and Vernel Singleton, who was my roommate. Shaq hung with other guys like Dennis Tracey, a white guard who later became Shaq's personal assistant after he went to the NBA. We had our moments, talking and laughing together, but we weren't close.

After we both got to the NBA, I realized Shaq was still holding some sort of grudge. A teammate, the late Bison Dele (formerly

Brian Williams), confirmed it when we played the Orlando Magic, Shaq's first NBA team. He said Shaq had refused to call me by the name I chose for myself, which indicated to Bison that he didn't much care for me.

"Oh, really?" I said. "Oh, I didn't know it was like that."

But I could tell our relationship was different. When we would encounter each other, he would be somewhat distant — way more distant than you might expect former college teammates to be. Then I was told he described me as a ball hog in a book, something about me never seeing a shot I didn't like. I let it go, figuring he's young and emotional. I thought in time he'd come around. I believe I was right — time has mellowed any edge in his feelings toward me. During my NBA controversy, he was a supporter of mine, and he has continued to say positive things about me in recent years. I also saw that throughout his career, there seemed to be a trend of him having issues with shooting guards who matched his shine: Penny Hardaway in Orlando, Kobe Bryant in Los Angeles, Dwyane Wade in Miami. When I saw that, I decided that there was no need for me to take it personal. Besides, with all the suffering and hardship in the world, it's just not worth it to me to dwell on stuff like that.

Even though I had been considered the top freshman in the country, I didn't want to experience any letdown going into the second season. I increased the intensity of my workouts.

Maurice Williamson did an interview (with the YouTube channel Beyond the Legacy) during which he talked about the time he went to the gym at about 10:30 or 11:00 one night to work on his game and was shocked to see me there: "Me being cocky from the East Coast, I'm thinking there's no southern basketball player that was better than me, especially at the guard position. . . . I go to the gym one night by myself to get some shots up. On the other side of the court was Mahmoud Abdul-Rauf. . . . I'm looking down at him;

he's making shots, I'm making shots. So I said, *'Let me see how good he really is.'* I read all the hype about him—McDonald's All American, player of the year in Mississippi. I asked him, 'Let's play one on one.' . . . We played one on one for almost an hour. And this guy was unbelievable. I never saw somebody shoot as well as he was shooting, outside of my father. Within that hour, I probably won one or two games, and we were playing to eleven. I can't recall exactly how many games we played, but let's just say it was a lot of games. . . . Once I thought I figured him out, he would pull something else out his hat. . . . I had to come to grips with reality—there was somebody better than me."

Now I don't remember Mo winning any games, but I guess it's possible. Ha!

Going into my second season, we were getting a great deal of preseason buzz. I was returning after a record-setting freshman season, plus we were adding the number one recruit in the nation, Shaquille, and we had Stanley and Mo eligible to play, along with Vernel and Wayne Sims coming back. The expectations for LSU were off the charts; preseason polls put us at number two in the nation.

During preseason practices, I think Coach Brown purposely avoided having Shaq and Stanley compete against each other. He was trying to build up a camaraderie and even affection between them, so he started them out usually on the same squad. If they began as practice opponents, it easily could have turned into animosity and even hatred. Sometimes you have to concentrate on building people up. I would have to get on Stanley sometimes. Shaq was always hungry to get the ball, but Stanley acted like he could take it or leave it. He didn't have the same level of hunger. One day, I told him, "Stanley, man, if you just put the work in, brother, you could name your price."

His response literally brought tears to my eyes. He looked at me and said, "Chris, man, I appreciate you. But I'm hardheaded. I ain't gonna listen."

Stanley was one of the nicest dudes you'd ever meet; it choked me up to hear him talk about himself that way. He was talented, but he didn't seem to have a strong interest in playing basketball. He just wanted to make a nice living and take care of his family. He didn't have the passion to dominate like Shaquille. Sometimes Coach Brown would tell me I needed to push him.

"Stanley, what are you doing?" I said to him on more than one occasion. "Shaquille is killing you out there. You gonna let him do that to you?"

He'd then dominate Shaq at practice. Stanley was actually bigger than Shaq at the time. Posting him up in the paint: *Pop. Pop. Pop.* But then he'd disappear for the next three practices. He'd show you just enough game to let you know, "Hey, if I wanted to, well, you see I can." It created in us a yearning to see him do that every time.

I was having my own challenges at this time with weight gain related to Tourette. Because of the Haldol, I was 185 pounds at the start of my freshman year, but I still averaged 30.2 points a game that first season, technically out of shape. I wonder what I would have done if I was a sleek 155. I'm sure I would have been quicker and more explosive. I decided that I needed to get off the Haldol. I mentioned it to Miss Lil, Coach Jenkins's wife. One day she came to LSU with another woman, Jo Evans, both beautiful people. These two extremely generous white ladies scooped me up and drove me all the way to Houston to see a doctor named Yankovic. He was a neurological specialist. They put me up in a hotel that night, and the next day we went to the doctor. He prescribed two different drugs, Prozac and Prolixin. He told me they wouldn't have the same side effects of Haldol, which made me hungry, thirsty, and sleepy and therefore made me gain weight. Instead, he said, I would lose weight.

During the summer, I had an epiphany and decided I wasn't going to take any drugs; I was going to go it on my own, drug-free. Figure out how to control the Tourette without any chemicals, which didn't seem to stop the tics anyway. I discovered how to manage Tourette syndrome with prayer, exercise, rest, reflection, watching what I eat, paying attention to how my body responds when I eat, and staying away as much as possible from pharmaceutical drugs. I have to be careful about what I eat because I know certain foods will trigger it. I love nuts, but if I eat too many they're going to make my heart rate go up and make my tics a bit more explosive. This also can happen with certain sugars.

Eating too much can also be a trigger. I don't want to eat to get full; I eat to feel satisfied. There's a tradition in Islam of a full belly being one-third food, one-third liquid, and one-third air. I try to use that as a model. I've learned that certain activities can help as well, such as sex and reading.

I'm pleased to say that I haven't touched any pharmaceutical drugs related to Tourette syndrome since before my sophomore year at LSU.

While playing ball that summer before my sophomore year, I broke my ankle. I had to wear a cast for several weeks. But I was committed to losing weight, even with the cast. I had a bathroom in my room that had one of those timed lights that would make the room very hot. I would go in the bathroom wearing a heavy cotton warm-up suit and I would shadowbox for hours at a time. Punching. Jabbing. Bobbing and weaving. I would come out drenched in sweat.

I heard that grapefruit juice was good for burning fat, so I drank it by the gallon. I ate cans of tuna fish without anything added, no mayonnaise, no eggs. When the cast finally came off, I started a routine of running, doing miles every day. After all that, I started the season at 169, in the best shape I'd been in several years.

I began with 37 points in a win against Southern Mississippi in the season opener. The night before the game, Vernel came to me, upset about stuff he said a guard from Southern Mississippi had been saying about me. "We gotta get them," Vernel said.

Apparently, the guy had been making fun of the Tourette. That was all the motivation I needed. I'm always intensely competitive, but that took it up a notch. As soon as I got the opening tip from Shaq, I went at the other team and that guard hard. I had to keep reminding myself to go fast but stay under control. My mindset was to go at this guy's throat, to make him pay for what he said. There was no bobbing and weaving, feeling out the opponent. It was attack mode from the start. I wanted to kill him. It didn't matter that he had no idea I knew what he'd said.

In our next game, we lost to Kansas by 6 points. They were a good team that made me earn every bucket. I finished with 32 in that one. During the game, Dick Vitale pronounced that I was the best player in America. That kind of stuff was great to hear, though it didn't necessarily help me on the court, putting an even bigger target on my back. But I had grown used to the target.

Then we had a series of "warm-ups" against overmatched opponents like McNeese State, Lamar, Northwestern State, and Hardin-Simmons. We beat McNeese by 36, Lamar by 40, Northwestern State by 10, and Hardin-Simmons by 34.

Before our next game against Texas in Austin, I heard through the grapevine that Travis Mays, their star guard, was talking noise about me and about our team. I'm not sure if he was or not, but at that point it didn't even matter. The result was that the rumors put me in the kill mindset. We were ranked eleventh in the nation before the game. We beat them by 11, 124–113. I finished with 50 points. I felt good about that one. It was my fourth game above 50 in a little bit more than one season.

Our five-game winning streak was broken by Mississippi State, who beat us 87–80. That loss stung because that was the crowd yelling at Shaq, "Go back to Africa, boy!" I played that game in a state of simmering outrage. During the game, Coach Brown put me in a tough situation. He was pissed off at some of the guys, so during a huddle he said, "Chris? Get the ball and don't pass to nobody. Shoot everything."

I came down and shot a few times even though I was getting double- and triple-teamed. I made them, but it felt weird because I saw that a couple of guys were open. One time I passed and looked at the coach in apology, as if to say, "My bad." But I didn't like being told to play like that. Yes, I took a lot of shots, but I've always been of the mind that I score because my team needs me to score. I'm not the kind of dude who's going to go out and see if I can get 70 just because we're playing a weaker team. If I think I got the shot, I'm going to take it. But sometimes you have to keep your teammates in the rhythm, especially if you feel you can get yours whenever you want it. I need them to run the floor hard, to set hard picks, to take open shots, because I know I'm going to need them down the road. It can't be all about me if we're going to win. If they're cold, when I'm being triple-teamed and I pass to them, they're going to feel awkward because they are out of rhythm.

We brought the game into overtime after I hit a three-pointer. But we couldn't keep up in overtime. I finished that Mississippi State game with 40. Next, we reeled off five wins in a row against some tough squads: Auburn, Tennessee, Kentucky, Vanderbilt, and Notre Dame. We lost to Alabama, a loaded team that had Robert Horry, Melvin Cheatum, and a bunch of other long, lanky guys who

matched up well against us. We lost to Georgia and beat Florida
before we took on UNLV. In addition to Stacey Augmon and Greg
Anthony, now they had added the dominating power forward Larry
Johnson to the squad. We were ranked sixteenth; UNLV was ranked
fifth. UNLV came into our gym while we were still practicing with
a shocking level of arrogance. They walked into the arena like they
owned the place, imposing themselves on our scheduled time and
space. They just had this swagger about them. We felt they were
sending a message—that they didn't respect us. We were looking at
them like, "Are you serious right now?" We went back to our dorm
rooms that night motivated to knock down some of that cockiness.

It was a close game, just like it was the previous year when
we upset them. I finished with 35 points in our 107–105 victory.
We were flying high, completing our seven-game winning streak
with wins against twentieth-ranked Loyola Marymount (who had
two of the nation's leading scorers, Bo Kimble and Hank Gathers),
Mississippi State, Auburn, and Tennessee (who had Allan Houston).

The Auburn game was the only one in my two years at LSU
in which I didn't score in double figures, and there's a story behind
that. I heard that guys on my team were complaining that I was
shooting too much and they weren't getting enough shots. I got
pissed. The same thing had happened back in high school; this time
my reaction was pretty much the same. I decided in the Auburn
game that I wasn't going to shoot. My thinking was, I went out and
worked my behind off every single day. I tried to play the game the
way it should be played. It was always a matter of pride with me,
since fourth grade, that I could get my shot off against anybody, no
matter how tough a defender he was. That's why I worked on a wide
variety of shots; that's why I worked on different release points, different footwork to create space. Because of all this, shots came easier
to me than to some of my teammates. All the time, just like high

school, I got coaches telling me to keep shooting. And my teammates were gonna complain that I wasn't passing them the ball enough? It seemed like every dang year somebody was developing some sensitivity, getting up in his feelings and wanting to run his mouth and complain. So against Auburn, I did nothing but pass. In the end, I had just 9 points. I was amused when, during the next game against Tennessee, analysts said that I was in some sort of slump in the Auburn game.

I was excited to play high-flying Loyola Marymount because I heard they had a real run-and-gun style. That was confirmed as soon as the game started. They would grab the ball out of the net after we scored and then take off, like a constant track meet. Before we could take a breath, they were already up the court. When they got a rebound, they were already leaking out. We had to adjust quick. Coach did a lot of subbing that game, but I wanted to stay in there. I love challenges, and this was right up my alley. In the end, I scored 34 and we won in overtime, 148–141. Yeah, you read that right. That was a higher point total than you'd find in most NBA games. Hank Gathers had 48 and Bo Kimble had 32, but it wasn't enough to overcome our squad. Shaq had a triple-double, with a ridiculous 12 blocks in the game.

We closed out the regular season with a tough SEC schedule, going 6–3 against SEC opponents. We finished the regular season with a record of 21–7, ranked nineteenth in the nation. But we lost in the first round of the SEC tournament to Auburn, 78–76. We got a bit further in the NCAA tournament, winning in the first round against Villanova. But our season ended with a second-round loss to Georgia Tech.

I was again selected as SEC Player of the Year, though my average dropped a bit to 27.8 points per game, and as first team All-American.

Prior to the NCAA tournament, guys weren't happy about how things were going. Some were even talking about transferring. I tried to explain that we should just go out and take care of our business on the floor and deal with these particulars afterward. But I understood if guys wanted to leave. Besides, I already had decided I was leaving LSU to move on to my next challenge: the NBA.

CHAPTER 13

While I was a student at LSU, my close connection to the religion of my childhood continued. Over the course of my day, I still would pause at times to thank God for everything in my life and to ask God to forgive me, to guide me, to strengthen me, to watch over my family and the people I loved. If I was driving a car, I turned off the radio if I was passing by a church. I went to church on occasion, but not regularly. Stepping into church would change me, at least temporarily. It would prick my conscience, make me pledge to be a better person, a better servant of God. A lot of it was laced with a fear factor—if you don't do this, you're going to hell. My thinking was, *I gotta get myself together because it could be my last day on Earth.* I was always hyperconscious of that. If I left this realm right now, where would I go? My answer was always negative: I wouldn't make it; I'd be going to hell. When I tried to be good, I felt like society was always pulling me in another direction. I was in a constant tug-of-war over my own soul. I'd straighten up and be good for a sec, then be enticed by women, money, always something.

My guilt was constantly bouncing around in my head—not just about things like sex but also about basketball. I'd pray to God for forgiveness, because even though I worked harder than anybody I knew, I constantly felt like I could be doing more, like I was disap-pointing God by not utilizing my talents to the fullest. I'm extremely hard on myself—a trait that has continued over the years. I'm always thinking, *You should do more. You should do more. You've been given all of this, man. Why are you wasting so much time?*

I also battled with the question of whether I was doing all of this to please God, or was it all for fame? And what's the best way to please God?

Guys who knew me were aware that I wasn't the type of dude to curse. I'd hear them say it sometimes: "Chris ain't drinking." "Chris ain't smoking." "Chris ain't cursing." I would find a private place on a bench somewhere after training, or sitting on steps, or on my front porch at home, and I would just think. Ponder. Often, I'd be thinking about dying.

What intensified when I got to LSU was the questioning of things about Christianity that I had been taught. I began to question the concept of the Trinity: the Father, the Son, the Holy Ghost. Then Jesus died on the cross. But how can you kill God? And how can three separate things be the same thing? When I was younger and I had questions, I would always get the same response from the adults: "You just got to believe—and you can't question God."

I would attend church when I felt like I needed to go, like when my conscience was getting the best of me. *I need to go. I need to go.* But it wasn't something pressing down on me. Ironically, the desire to attend church led to one of the two most pivotal events in my religious evolution, both occurring while I was at LSU.

One Sunday afternoon, I was driving around Baton Rouge when I came upon an enormous Baptist church. All of a sudden, I was struck with a desire to go inside. It felt like I was being pushed inside the church. I walked in and saw a white pastor at the pulpit and mostly white people sitting on the pews that went all the way around the large building, which was in the design of an amphitheater, like the Roman Colosseum. I had never seen such a church before in my life. I caught some of the service, though I can't recall what subject the pastor was preaching about. As I sat there, I could tell by the way people were looking at me that many of them recognized me. I got more attention than probably any athlete at LSU at the time; it wasn't surprising that people around Baton Rouge would know who I was.

At the end of the service, I was approached by a smallish white woman, probably in her late thirties. I saw that she was accompanied by a young boy, maybe about eight or nine years old. I was sitting there by myself, minding my business, contemplating what I had just heard. I just wanted to be able to relax and let the moment wash over me. I was a bit startled when the woman spoke to me. "Can we pray for you?" she asked.

My first thought was, *What gave you the impression that I need praying over?* But I didn't want to seem ungrateful, so I acquiesced.

"Okay," I said. I'm pretty sure the doubt was evident in my tone of voice.

"Can my son pray over you?" she asked.

I thought *she* was going to be doing the praying. But no, it was to be the little boy. I said, "Sure," though I wasn't certain what was about to happen.

I was taken aback when this little white boy put his hand on my head. What he did next threw me: he started speaking in tongues. *What in the world?*

At first I just bowed my head as I listened to him. But the longer the unintelligible sounds coming out of his mouth went on, I got increasingly disturbed. I kind of went limp, now hanging my head in resignation. However, my mind was racing. *Are you serious right now?*

I didn't want to embarrass him by halting him in the middle of his prayer and removing his hand from my head. But I was extremely disturbed by the whole scene. Since I was a child back at Morning Star Baptist Church in Gulfport, I had always had many questions about the practice of speaking in tongues. If God wanted to communicate with me, wouldn't he do it in a language I could understand? And if you're trying to pray over me, shouldn't I be privy to the words you're using? If the point is to lift me up and inspire me, how will I know what you're praying about when it's coming out in gibberish? With the odd sounds coming out of the boy's mouth, I had to ask myself: Was this for me or for him? In the Bible, the Quran, the Talmud, it is clear that God sends messages in a language people understand.

That experience flattened the tires for me even more with Christianity. I began to pray to God to guide me to something that made sense to me, that I could live and die with. I was generally confused by all the information swirling around out there, with few trusted places I could go for answers.

The second pivotal event came by way of Coach Brown. One day Coach handed me a book and said he thought I'd find it interesting. It was *The Autobiography of Malcolm X*, written with Alex Haley. Believe it or not, I had never heard of Malcolm X when I got to LSU. That wasn't the kind of information you were gonna be taught in the public schools of Mississippi, and as I said earlier, my household growing up wasn't a place where we were surrounded by books on Black history or anything else. I wasn't much of a reader, but I couldn't put the book down. I would be itching to finish training on the court so I could get back to the book. This was a total reversal of the usual order of things. Normally I'd be yearning to run away from a book so I could get back on the court.

The most immediate effect of Malcolm's words was to make me angry. The book made me look at white people differently. I developed a mistrust and a dislike for white people, though I had to pretend on the surface like nothing had changed. Even the ones who were nice to me, like Coach Brown, I began to look at sideways, which was ironic considering he had given me the book. In his early days, Malcolm went hard in making the case that the white man was the devil, which was a tenet of the Nation of Islam. The Nation's philosophy didn't totally make sense to me, but it began to open my eyes to the world around me. When I took a closer look at the systems Malcolm was talking about — the financial system, the legal system, the educational system, the political system, et cetera — he was right that they all were controlled by white people. White people who smiled to your face and then enslaved you. Or they smiled to your face and then cheated you. After that book, I was out there shaking hands, smiling, doing interviews — and all the while looking at every single person with all kinds of suspicion in my mind, thinking, *I don't really know if I can trust you.* I started calling white people "honkies" and "crackers."

I befriended a Catholic priest named Father Bayhi, whom Coach Brown sometimes invited to pray with us before games and tag along on the road with us. I would have discussions with him about religion and the like. I was still trying to rock with Christianity, so I'd put a cross in my sock or shoe before games, even while I was reading Malcolm. In a very vague sense, I was starting to open my mind up to other belief systems outside of Christianity, such as Islam, but my thinking still was all over the place. Part of the issue was that I grew up being taught so intensely about Christ and the Bible that I was fearful about leaving that behind me, even if other things were starting to make more sense. I was afraid that perhaps I wasn't getting the full story about belief systems like Islam, that maybe I was being tricked by crafty language or something. So, I held on to what I was familiar with, at least for the time being. I was still too scared to step away from everything I knew and embrace something new.

Malcolm had qualities I didn't have but I wanted. He was very knowledgeable, well-read, articulate, courageous. He didn't seem to care what people thought. He wasn't afraid to speak his conscience. I felt like I wasn't on that level, but I wanted to be. I desperately wanted some of what he had. Inspired by Malcolm, I slowly began to make changes in my life. I began by learning how to tell people no. I started to become more self-assured about speaking up if I saw things that were wrong, behavior that was wrong, situations that were unfair. Before, I was too hesitant to say something for fear of what people would think of me. I didn't want to be that way, but I couldn't help it.

I was still frustrated by my performance in the classroom at LSU. Like everything else, habits have to be formed to make them consistent. I just could not develop the habit of pushing myself academically. I couldn't call on my basketball discipline and apply it to my schoolwork. I would get mad at myself and vow to be better, especially at the start of each semester.

Man, I'm gonna try to be an A student this semester. Man, I'm going to really buckle down and get my work done.

I would start out with the best of intentions, but just like in high school I wouldn't be able to sustain it. It actually confounded me. I would scold myself all the time: *Man, you can go out there and shoot a basketball in all sorts of weather conditions. You can wake up in the dark and shoot for hours at a time. For years. What's wrong with you – why can't you apply that focus to school?*

At some point during my freshman year, when asked to declare a major, I put down business management, which was a typical major for an athlete. But I never took any classes toward the major. There were many aspects of my academic career that I would prefer to forget. When I first got on campus, school administrators brought me upstairs in one of the academic buildings and put me through an experience that I found humiliating. A white woman told me to sit down. She handed me a book, pointed to a passage, and asked me to read it. It didn't take me long to figure out what was going on: they were checking to see if I could read and how I read. Was I just reciting words, or could I define them and think through the material? I was stunned. Like, really?

I made it through the passage smoothly, pronouncing the words correctly, getting into a nice flow. So far, so good. Anybody listening would think, *Oh, this guy has this under control.* But then she started asking me questions about what I had read. Comprehension had never been my strong suit. With the Tourette perpetually distracting me, I often had to read paragraphs several times to get their meaning.

"What does this word mean?" she asked, pointing to a word in the passage.

"Oh. Um, I don't know."

"Okay. What does this word mean?" She pointed again.

"I don't know," I responded.

"What about this?"

I felt the nervous perspiration starting to build up. It was a familiar feeling: shame. I was embarrassed, like I was being exposed as the fraud that I often felt I was. After the third question, my whole demeanor changed. I got a bit hostile.

"Well, what can you tell me about the story?" she asked. "What did you get out of the story?"

I was just reading. I wasn't even thinking about what I had been reading. I could have tried to comprehend more as I read, but it wasn't my focus. Asked to read aloud, I was trying to get that right.

That was easily one of the lowest moments in my academic career. After that encounter, they decided to put me in a remedial reading class where we spent most of our time working on reading comprehension. On a college campus. I couldn't believe it. It brought back all those feelings of humiliation from seventh grade special education. Even the class I attended was like the special education class, tucked away in the corner of a building on the ground level. In fact, it wasn't even a real classroom; it was more like an office. There were about five or six other people in the "class" with me. I wasn't the only Black man, but the group was a diverse collection of Black and white, with one or two women. I'm not sure how the other people got in the class; none of them were elite athletes, so it wasn't a sports thing. In retrospect, I wonder how they managed to get into LSU if they weren't elite athletes.

I had long ago convinced myself that I was lacking in intellectual capabilities, so while the class was embarrassing, it did little to worsen what was already a pretty low self-perception. But I didn't tell any of my teammates I was in a remedial reading class. That created a weird dynamic where I was out there breaking records on the court, appearing on television every week, signing autographs and shaking hands, and presenting myself as a confident, fairly articulate guy, but at the same time needing help with my reading skills, in a class learning things I should have learned a long time ago.

In many of my other classes, such as sociology or political science, I would often doze off. In between waking up early to go to practice, training, and playing many night games in other cities, being an athlete took its toll. It was like having a nine-to-five job. I'd be sitting in class asking myself why I needed to know this stuff. I just needed to be able to count well enough to balance a budget. Why did I need to know history? It's just something that's in the past. I'm still incredulous at how uninterested and distant I was from learning, from understanding the value of educating myself on a wide variety of issues.

I was reluctant to join any student groups or ask classmates for help with anything. I didn't want to possibly reveal my inadequacies. I was filled with insecurities when it came to that stuff.

I had a political science professor who always made me think in his class. He would inspire me to want to go and do more reading. He knew how to pique my curiosity. But all that would get overwhelmed by basketball. My desire to be great always won the day, because I would start getting worried that if I spent too much time on academics, it might take away from basketball. I couldn't risk making it to the NBA on reading a couple more books. In my mind, that calculation didn't work out in my favor. Basketball was my bread and butter.

I still felt a similar way about messing around with women — that I couldn't let myself get distracted. At LSU I would effectively tell them, maybe in slightly more delicate language, "I can date you, but if you become high-maintenance, sugar, you gotta go. If you don't understand what I'm saying, you gotta go. I don't care how beautiful you are, who is in your family, how much money you got. I don't care how great the sex is. You gotta go."

Understand, I wasn't saying this in an ugly way. I was diplomatic about it. But I needed to make sure women understood what I was saying. There were a lot of beautiful ladies on campus; by no means was I practicing celibacy. But I wasn't going to let women and sex get in the way of my workouts. Most of my time was spent at the gym. I was usually either coming from the gym or going to the gym. If somebody saw me out at a party, they acted like they'd seen a ghost. And I would risk that only if I had a particularly good month of training.

But then one day, everything changed in an instant. You know how people say when it hits, you will know it? It felt like everything in existence, from the molecules and atoms to the climate and wind flow to the animals and planetary structures, was all aligned at that moment to move me in her direction. It was hard to think of anything or anyone else.

CHAPTER 14

I was walking across campus one afternoon after a class, headed back to the dorm so that I could get ready for a workout in the gym. I was minding my business, my head probably focused on an upcoming game. And that's when I saw her. She was a beautiful, light-skinned Black girl, about 5'5" with long goldish hair and an exceptionally curvy body that was evident even though she was wearing regular loose-fitting college student gear. In the vernacular of Black dudes in the 1980s, she was a "redbone." *Oh my God, who in the world is that?*

She had a walk that could stop the globe from spinning; it was absolutely aesthetically mesmerizing. I just had to find out who this girl was. I had to get close to her. I had to inhale the same air she breathed, to hear her voice carried by the wind to my ears. As she walked past me, it was hard not to keep looking at her (without being obvious), which was very much out of character for me. I've always been more old-school about my approach to women. I might nod my head and keep it moving. In this case, I nodded at her, but I wasn't sure she saw me. I watched her walk away, entranced by the way her body moved. *Maaan, this girl was nice!*

I felt it in my chest as she walked away: a feeling I had never experienced. I had gotten zapped. Not to sound possessive, but I had to have her.

I couldn't stop thinking about her. I didn't even know her name, but I started praying to God. *Please, God, please let this woman be a part of my life.*

I saw her in approximately the same spot several more times. I nodded to her and she nodded back. But I still hadn't gotten the words to approach her.

One day I was sitting around talking to some of the football players. I started describing this beautiful girl I kept seeing on campus.

"There's this lady, and I don't know her name, but man, she's so fine. She's light-skinned, thick." I told them where I thought she stayed on campus.

Darrell, the brother of one of my friends on the football team, looked at me and nodded. "Oh, you're talking about Kim," he said. "I date her friend Tiffany."

And that's the moment I first learned the name of my future wife. Kim.

"What? You gotta be kidding me." I asked him if she was seeing anybody. I think he shrugged. He wasn't certain if she was.

"Man, I'mma set y'all up!" he said.

Darrell called his girlfriend and set it up for Kim to meet me at the hilltop next to Graham Hall, their dorm. She showed up; we were introduced. I liked her even more when I actually started talking to her. We talked for at least three or four hours that day. Toward the end, I asked her if she was seeing anyone. She hesitated.

"Yes, I am," she said. "But I'm getting ready to end it."

She started telling me about her relationship problems. The guy wasn't an LSU student; he was back home in New Orleans, where she was from.

"I didn't mean to interrupt anything," I said. I was trying to sound like a southern gentleman, but I was lying. I definitely did intend to interrupt her relationship with dude—but only if that was something she wanted.

She shook her head. "No, I was already in the process," she said. "I'm getting ready to end it."

That was the start of our love affair. We started spending more time together, doing a lot of talking. She told me she was coming to the Georgetown game, which was at the end of January. When I first came onto the floor for the game, I tried to find her in the stands, but I didn't see her. I had to tell myself to let go of the distractions and concentrate on the game.

The relationship deepened over the next couple of months, but we weren't intimate yet. She still hadn't ended it with the guy in New Orleans. After the team went to Arizona for the NCAA tournament, I got a call from her in my room right after we lost to UTEP in the first round. The timing of the call wasn't the greatest. Coach Carse was in my room talking to me.

"I got something to tell you!" she said excitedly on the other end.

"Yeah? What is it?"

"I broke up with him!" she said.

"Okay," I responded. I was trying to act all cool, but inside I was doing somersaults. "All right. We'll talk when I get back. I'm here talking to Coach."

When I got back, our relationship took a big step forward. We were intimate for the first time; soon everybody on campus knew we were together. A few months later, I held my breath and got a rental car to drive Kim to Gulfport to see where I grew up. And meet my mom.

On the way there, I gave her a warning. "Listen, she might act a certain way toward you. Just ignore her. This is about you and me. This is about our relationship. I'm just forewarning you right now. She does that to pretty much everybody that I'm trying to see."

As predicted, my mother gave Kim a bit of a cold shoulder. I saw it coming a mile away. In the past, it felt like she befriended girls after I broke up with them. I could understand, *kinda*. She was a typical mother who thought no woman was good enough for her little boy. However, I thought Jackie Jackson took it to extremes. And to compound her normal suspicions, I now had a national profile with a host of accolades and records attached to my name, bringing significant attention from the NBA. My mother couldn't be certain if this girl loved her son or loved *the idea* of her son—and where her son likely was soon going.

After we left my mother, I brought Kim to the beach. We walked along the boardwalk and put our feet in the water while we held hands. It was extremely romantic—so romantic that I was moved to make it official.

"Listen, we've been seeing each other for a little while now. I want to make this official. I want you to be my woman. And I'll be your man."

It wasn't a proposal of marriage—more like a proposal of serious girlfriend-boyfriend. A proposal of exclusivity. Like everybody in Baton Rouge—probably everybody in the country, or at least college basketball fans—she most likely assumed I was going pro in another year or so. She didn't act like that prospect worried her in any way. We were together, we were in love, and we had had conversations about both of us wanting to have a family someday. I shared with her my vision of my future family and how it was my inspiration for training. I think she knew if we stayed together, she would be the one, the woman who would become my wife and the mother of my children. She never pushed me, never gave me any ultimatums, like that she needed a ring if we were going to stay together. Nothing like that.

As we headed toward the end of the semester, we were solidly in love and looking forward to a future together. I was excited about the prospect of starting my own family, something I had been dreaming about since I was a child, toiling away on those courts in Gulfport. I was also pleased to be inching closer to being able to help my family and my community.

At LSU, I became even more obsessed with the pain and sorrow I saw in communities I would come across, particularly Black communities. It was a continuation of the feelings I had back in elementary school, when I'd sit in front of the television with tears streaming down my face as I watched those infomercials about starving kids with flies buzzing around their faces and their bellies distended. I would be sobbing and praying, *God, please help these people! Please put me in a position to help them, to benefit their lives!*

My keen sensitivity to suffering would have me weeping at movies or television shows when I felt like someone was being taken advantage of or made to endure pain. Because of my childhood, I know what that feels like, to not know where your next meal is coming from. I don't ever want to lose my connection to that feeling. For me, it also had a connection to my relationship with God, praying for relief for not only myself but others as well. My grandmother and my uncle always impressed upon me the importance of praying for others—that you should pray for others more than you pray for yourself. And don't just leave it at that. You should move toward the things you are praying for. For me, that always meant praying for children, elderly men and women, the sick, the impoverished, the oppressed, and even those doing well, because there are challenges we all experience. It coincides with that Gandhi quote: "The best way to find yourself is to lose yourself in the service of others." When you pray for others, when you give, it comes back to you. You're blessed more if you give for the right reason. This has been the thinking I have carried with me throughout my life.

Even though I was living in a dorm, eating three nice meals a day, taking trips all over, and being featured on national television broadcasts, I still had a soft spot in my heart for the disadvantaged. I know what it feels like to be cold and hungry. It tears me up how we have become so desensitized to suffering. We see it all around us: death, murder, poverty, famine. The more we see, it feels like the more desensitized we get. This society has become so focused on pulling your own self up, right? This sense of narcissism and individualism. There's a verse in the Quran where Allah tells us that to take one life unjustly, it's as though you have "killed all mankind." Allah said oppression is worse than killing someone, because when you kill someone, it's over — you can't do anything to that person anymore. Yes, the family is affected, but the act is done. However, when you oppress someone, it has more of a generational effect. It stretches over years and years, affecting many lives.

I always kept these things in mind as I started to experience more privilege. When you become wealthy, hanging with certain groups of people, you can become disconnected. It's not always intentional; it's just the way things often are. I've always utilized various means to stay connected, especially prayer. When I was in the NBA and when I traveled overseas, as soon as I put down my bags, I would head to the ghettos. I wanted to know the rough areas, how people were living and dying in those places. Someone even wrote a story about this practice of mine when I was in the league. I never intended for this to be publicized, but you never know who is paying attention and how it impacts them.

In addition to all that, I have a constant reminder of suffering that won't let me rest: Tourette syndrome. Tourette is constantly letting me know, *Hey, look, man, you might be all this, but guess what? I got some control over you.* Tourette won't let me be calm for even a minute. It's constantly humbling me, not letting me get too loose and relaxed.

I never had the luxury of being arrogant because I had a constant thought in the back of my mind: *How bad a dude could you possibly be? You can't even control yourself.*

CHAPTER 15

T*o go or not to go?* That was the question. I was a two-time SEC Player of the Year, a two-time consensus first team All-American, widely seen as perhaps the top player in the country. Why stay?

Initially I was nervous about telling Coach Brown I was thinking of leaving. I didn't want to say anything during the season. You never know how a coach will react to something like that. I didn't want to risk him messing with my playing time, thinking he needed to move on and get the next man ready.

But I was talking about it with my teammates. As we moved through the season, I mentioned it to a few guys I was closer to, like my roommate, Vernel. However, what sealed the deal for me was when I took a rare trip home during the season to see my mother. I didn't go home a lot during the season. I didn't want to be distracted; I didn't want all the pats on the back while I was in the middle of it. I just wanted to stay down in that basement gym on campus, working on my game as much as possible. I felt that too much time in Gulfport and I may lose focus. When I went back, I would mainly spend time with my mom, maybe take a quick drive through Soria City. But I tried to be in and out in a few hours.

On this particular trip, which I took in the middle of my sophomore season, I went to the refrigerator to get something to drink, and there was nothing inside. Empty. I was devastated. I was up on campus, eating at dining halls where I could go back as many times as I wanted, and my mother and Omar literally had nothing to eat. I felt an anger and also a shame course through me. I went into the bathroom, my mind reeling. As I was washing my hands, I leaned on the sink — and the whole basin fell to the floor. I was stunned. I knew there wasn't much to this house where I had spent so much of my childhood, but I didn't expect the thing to be literally falling apart.

I walked out of the bathroom in a funk. "To hell with this, man, I'm done!"

My mother was in the kitchen, sitting at the little brown table. "What?" she asked.

"I'm not staying in school! I'm leaving!"

I saw her head drop. My rant had saddened her. But my mind was made up in that moment. I was angry. And I felt guilty about how I was living compared with my mother and little brother. I didn't like school anyway, so the idea of leaving LSU and going on to make millions of dollars wasn't that complicated. LSU had merely been a transition for me anyway, a layover on the way to my final destination. I wasn't concentrating much on my classes, still memorizing what I needed to make the grade. I began to worry about the uncertainty of it all. *What if something happens to me, man? What will I do? How will I take care of my family?* No, I needed to make this move.

One day Coach Brown summoned me to his office. "I heard that you were considering going to the NBA," he said. Apparently word had jumped from my teammates to the coach. I shouldn't have been surprised; people can't help themselves.

"Coach, I'd love to stay," I said. "But I'm concerned about my family. I gotta feed my family. I don't know what the future holds. I don't want to think about if something happens to me and I had this opportunity and I didn't take it. One of my major reasons for playing is to take care of my family, to help people. And I'm in a position right now to do that."

Coach looked at me for a moment without speaking. The memory of the scene is so clear in my mind, like it happened yesterday.

"Well, I tell you, this is what we're gonna do, Chris. For the rest of the season, we're going to run more plays for you. You do what you want to do out there."

He paused. What he said was amusing to me because he had already given me an unlimited green light to shoot whenever I wanted.

"I'm gonna call around and ask where people think you will go," he said, then nodded. "I agree. This is the best year for you to go."

I watched him closely. I wasn't completely buying what he was telling me. By this time, I had already absorbed Malcolm X's book. He wasn't aware, but I was in the middle of the phase where I looked at all white people like they were the devil. I wasn't necessarily showing this suspicion in my manner—I was still as cordial as I had been when I was around white people—but the information Malcolm had shared had a profound effect on me. I struggled with the question of whether Coach Brown was sincere. Did he really have my back like that? Or was I just a piece of property to him—a vehicle to get what he wanted? I was skeptical of what he was saying because a part of me felt like he should have been encouraging me to finish my education. He wasn't trying to sell that at all.

Even though I kind of wanted to hear him refer to my LSU education, it wouldn't have been a particularly strong selling point anyway. Once I had decided I was going to the league, my commitment to my classes and coursework, already weak to begin with, became almost nonexistent. I basically stopped going to class. When I called years later because I was contemplating going back to school to get the degree, the registrar's office told me my GPA when I left was the equivalent of a D. It looked bad, but I was actually surprised that I was passing. To be honest, I didn't think I deserved to pass any of those classes.

After telling me he was going to make some calls on my behalf, Coach Brown followed through on his word. In fact, I was in his office when he received a return call from a player whom many consider to be the greatest of all time: Michael Jordan. Coach put him on the speakerphone.

"Once you make a decision, approach it a hundred percent," M.J. said. "Don't look back."

Coach Brown called the Lakers legend and general manager Jerry West and a bunch of others. He gave me a report in his office: "They tell me you are going to be top five if you come out now." He studied me. "You should come out now."

I nodded. "Okay."

My next step was to find an agent. That was not a process I enjoyed. People were constantly promising me things, trying to sell me on things; it was hard to know whom to trust, who had my best interests at heart. It reminded me too much of the college recruiting process.

At one point I got a visit from an African American agent who met me at my dorm. When I think back on how I assessed him, I'm ashamed by what I was thinking. I was still a victim of the racial indoctrination that hammered away at Black kids from the South. Imagery and conditioning are very powerful. I saw how this guy was dressed, and I was taken aback by the overly casual way he presented himself. But most of all, I was indoctrinated to look at white people as being the authority. I didn't have much experience with Black agents; I was not sure a Black man could get as good a deal for me as a white agent. In retrospect, I didn't give the Black guy much of a chance. It still burns me up, how I was thinking back then. I now see it as a vivid example of the dangers of not being properly educated and of seeing the world through a painfully narrow lens.

In the end, I went with Eddie Miller, the Gulfport attorney who was my former AAU coach. I chose someone who was familiar, comfortable. Once I hired him, he advanced me some cash for spending money that I had to pay back when I got my big payday. He guided me as I went through the paces with a bunch of NBA teams. The psychological evaluations were the most excruciating. They would ask me questions that I found irritating, but I would have to hide my irritation. The worst questions were the ones related to Tourette.

"Do you think it's going to affect your play?"

I struggled to keep from exploding: *Did you not see the last two years? Did it look like it was affecting my play when I was one of the top scorers in the country? If anything, it made me better.*

I had had Tourette since I was a small child and throughout my entire basketball career. On the precipice of me joining the NBA, it seemed silly to ask me that question. Ask me if it affected me in school or something. Ask me whether I had outbursts where I maybe got violent or angry, things that they should be aware of. But don't ask me whether it would affect my basketball play. It made me look at these guys in a different way, like they weren't as savvy as I previously thought.

They asked the LSU coaches a lot of questions as well.

"How is he as a person?"

"Did he work hard?"

"Did he get along with people?"

Teams were very interested in my conditioning, but they all had different ways of investigating. In Miami, I met with the coach, and as players started coming in, I shot around with them. Glen Rice and a couple more guys came. Before I knew it, we were playing two-on-two, then three-on-three. We were playing, but we weren't really playing. The games weren't intense; they were more intended for us to get to know each other, to watch us interact. I guess they were assessing how I got along with the guys.

Charlotte was a lot more intense. They had me do a series of tough suicide drills, then they wanted to see if I could make shots when I was tired. I thought it was a good process. It's easy to make shots at that level when you're rested up. You should be able to make those shots. But what happens when you're spent? What types of adjustments do you make to be more efficient with your movement? What does your body language look like? Are you going to slump over, almost like a pout, like you're ready to give up? Or are you still going to ask for the ball? Are you the type of player who says, "Give it to me and I'll fight through it"? The answers to those questions say a lot about you. In the third and fourth quarters, when you're tired, it's easy to start getting frustrated, to allow your anger to get the best of you. You start slumping over, compromising your technique. Maybe you start running away from the action. But for some players, you get pissed off and your anger pushes you harder. Even when I train guys today, I tell them, "Sure, you look good when you're rested. If I was a scout, I'd want to start looking at you when you get tired and winded, when you're breathing hard."

Dallas was maybe the most interesting visit. My new agent, Eddie Miller, made the trip with me. He didn't tell me until it was over that the Dallas guys didn't think I could hit the NBA three-pointer. He told me that as we got back into the car. After I heard that, the paces they put me through made a lot more sense. The coach who was running the workout had me run down the court full speed, stop on a dime behind the arc, and shoot it. When my first shot hit the front of the rim, I saw him look at Eddie Miller, almost as if he were saying, "Aha!" Miller just looked back at him with a smirk. I didn't think much of that exchange between them.

He had me do a bunch of different moves. Go full speed, go between your legs, go left, and shoot. Go between your legs, go right, and shoot. Go behind your back, go right, get to that spot over there, and shoot. And everything at full speed. After that first one fell short, the next twenty-five shots or so probably didn't even touch the rim. All net. Every single one of them.

When we were done, the coach walked over to me. "Out of all my years, I've never seen a shooting exhibition like that in my life," he said. He looked at Miller, shaking his head. "Man, I wish we were high enough in the draft to get him!"

Interestingly, considering where I landed, I didn't even visit Denver. I visited about a half dozen teams in total. Some were teams that were struggling, with bad win-loss records — teams that would likely be in the NBA lottery for the top college players. Some teams believed in picking the best player available with their first pick, while others typically looked to fill a pressing need. Starting in 1987, only the first three picks were determined by the lottery. Starting in 1990, my year, the team with the worst win-loss record had the best chance of landing the first pick because of the weighted system the league put in place.

On draft day, I sat alone in a hotel room in Manhattan. All the guys they thought would be top draft picks were there; the whole thing was televised. My agent offered to fly my family members into New York, but I decided against it. I don't even know whether I can adequately explain why. I'm just like that sometimes. Even though it was a draft and not a game, I wanted to stay focused. I didn't want any distractions around me. I'm still like that, even with my kids coming to see me play in the Big3 league. I didn't want to have to think about my family's needs and well-being instead of focusing on the matter at hand. In that room I needed moments of solitude, reflection, space to think. It was extremely emotional for me. I had been single-mindedly focused on this one thing since the age of nine, fixated on making it to the NBA to the exclusion of almost everything else. In many instances, to the exclusion of allowing pleasure in my life. I had one goal. I had no plan B. This was it. And now it was here: the day I had been dreaming about for twelve years. I wanted to sit and pray, to thank God for delivering me to this moment.

There was excitement but also nervousness and fear. For people on the outside, it looked like pure celebration. *Wow! This is the best!* But I was fighting my long-standing fears about something coming along to destroy everything, like with the Evans family on *Good Times.* New York is a huge city. Anything can happen. Maybe this was too good to be true. And I still had to fly back home. After that, I had to worry about basically starting all over again in a new city. I didn't need any more evidence of the uncertainty of it all than what had happened to Hank Gathers, the Loyola Marymount star whom I had battled against just a few months earlier in February. On March 4, a month and a day after we beat Loyola Marymount, Hank collapsed on the court during a game against Portland and was pronounced dead at the hospital. I was devastated by the news of his death. It reinforced for me the idea that nothing is guaranteed.

My emotions were all over the map. Of course, I was ecstatic, happy that I had finally made it. Or almost made it, that is. But I couldn't breathe easy until I got that first check and joined my new team. I still wasn't out of the ghetto.

I had gotten a phone call from the Denver Nuggets, telling me they planned to select me with the third pick. But I didn't put much stock in that; I had heard stories of players getting similar phone calls but then the team not taking them. I told them I appreciated the call. But I needed to hear NBA commissioner David Stern call out my name before I'd believe anything.

The New Jersey Nets took forward Derrick Coleman of Syracuse with the first pick. The Seattle SuperSonics went second and chose guard Gary Payton of Oregon State. I hadn't played against either of them in college. I actually had a lunch meeting with the Seattle brass, but I didn't get the sense that they were that interested in me. I left the meeting thinking it was probably a waste of time. When Commissioner Stern called my name with the third pick, announcing I was going to the Denver Nuggets, I felt an enormous sense of relief. On my way up to the stage, I stopped and hugged Coach Brown. Someone from the Nuggets gave me a Nuggets baseball cap that I put on my head. I was wearing a grayish double-breasted suit, somewhat oversized, as was the style in 1990. After I shook Stern's hand onstage, I returned to the back room and received a phone call from Nuggets management. They offered their congratulations, saying they were happy for me and looking forward to having me on the squad.

And that was it. My journey to the NBA had ended. I was about to step into the promised land. I was ecstatic, scared, excited, nervous. All of that. But I was ready, too. Little did I know of the backbreaking challenges that awaited me in the NBA.

took a few weeks to come to terms with Denver and actually sign a contract. We had to wait to see how much Coleman was going to get from the Nets. If we went too early and he got a whole lot more, then we would have shot ourselves in the foot. In the end, I signed a contract with Denver that was worth about $2 million a year. That number sounded fantastic, though I was about to be introduced to Uncle Sam.

"Don't look!"

As I was opening my first-ever paycheck from the Nuggets, I heard those words directed at me. It was Walter Davis, the NBA All-Star who was the career leading scorer for the Phoenix Suns before he joined the Nuggets in 1988. I turned to Sweet D, as we called him, to see what he was talking about.

"Don't look at the federal taxes and withholding," he said with a half smile.

Of course, when somebody tells you to not look at something, the first thing you do is to look. My eyes bulged. Immediately I got angry. The check amount of almost $80,000 had been nearly cut in half after taxes, down to just over $40,000. It was a painful wake-up call to my new life in this tax bracket. I was disturbed because I had very little trust in the system. I thought about how many people I could help with all those tens of thousands that I would be giving to the government, which I suspected would be primarily interested in helping the friends of President George H. W. Bush and his Republican Party rather than the people like those I left behind in Gulfport who needed it.

I had the option of getting one check per month or every two weeks. I chose the latter option. Even with the tax hit, it was hard to fathom the fact that I would be getting a check every two weeks for $40,000. Just months earlier, I needed to ask my coach to help me get something to eat if I got hungry after the dining halls closed. Just months earlier, I had looked into my mom's refrigerator and saw emptiness staring back at me.

Despite my pleasure from my sudden riches, I was not in a good place when I started workouts with the Nuggets. The team was in the midst of a major overhaul. Bernie Bickerstaff, who had been the coach of the Seattle SuperSonics—he was at the lunch meeting I had with Seattle before the draft—came in as president and general manager of the Nuggets. Coach Doug Moe, whose run-and-gun style perennially led the league in scoring, was out, replaced by Loyola Marymount coach Paul Westhead, whose team I had just beaten earlier in the year. This was not good news for me, because Moe apparently was the person in the Nuggets front office who wanted me; I would have likely been a great complement to his run-and-gun style. Though Westhead also used a high-scoring system at Loyola Marymount, producing two of the top scorers in the country in Bo Kimble and the late Hank Gathers, he and I just didn't mesh. I'm not sure why. I got the impression early on that he didn't want me there. And I wasn't coming in as the best version of myself.

I had started gaining a lot of weight in the off-season. I was depressed in this strange new city. I was stressed out. I wasn't used to snow and a winter gloominess that you didn't find in the South, even when it got cold. I didn't like this new environment. I hadn't yet caught up to the huge learning curve that NBA rookies encounter. I had to negotiate a new city and do all the grown-up stuff like find a place to live, pay my bills, get a car, get insurance. It didn't help that the team was awful. At the close of December, we had a record of

6–17. We didn't get a win until our third game of the season. I hadn't dreamed of any of this when I was in fourth grade.

But there was an enormous bright spot in those early months, something I was able to do for my mother to make a particular part of my dream come true: I surprised her and bought her a house.

Before I joined the Nuggets, I told my mother I wanted to take her for a drive. I had already talked to my agent about wanting to buy her a house. But I wanted it to be a complete surprise. As we drove around Gulfport, I told her that I was looking for a house for myself. My mother hadn't asked me for anything once I left for LSU, after we got past that recruiting ugliness. When I got drafted, she never gave me the impression that she was thinking, *Oh yeah, I'm about to have it made now. My son is gonna hook me up!* She was just happy for me.

I had a list of houses to look at. When we pulled up to each one, I asked her, "How about this house?"

With the first two she saw, she said she wasn't crazy about them. But when we pulled up in front of the third one, she said, "I like that. That's nice."

"Yeah, it is nice," I said. "I like it, too. I just hope that I'm able to get it."

As soon as I dropped her back home, I called my agent.

"Listen, man," I said. "I need to get that house ASAP. But I don't want my mother to know anything."

I told the same thing to my older brother, David. Miller helped me to secure the house when I was in Denver. I told David I would be relying on him to help me get the house furnished and decorated without Mom finding out. I wanted every detail to be run through me. The interior decorator would send me pictures, drawings, and ideas. I would give a thumbs-up or a thumbs-down. My goal was to have it walk-in ready, with linens, monogrammed towels, dishes, food in the refrigerator. I wanted her to be able to walk out of the house in Soria City and have to only bring some clothes with her.

In early November, we were ready for it to go down. The team was flying to Texas for a three-game swing through Dallas, Houston, and San Antonio. After we lost to Houston, the team gave me permission to fly home to Gulfport before I joined them in San Antonio for a night game the next day. It had to be a real quick trip to get this done. I was nervous about my time, nervous about everything going according to the plan. Just plain nervous. My family had arranged for the local television station WLOX to be at the house and chronicle the blissful event. As I walked into the new house, I was surprised to be greeted by a crowd congratulating me. Miller and my brother had invited a bunch of people to gather in the house to yell "Surprise!" when my mother appeared. They had the whole thing catered. I wasn't pleased about the size of the crowd, but I was too focused on everything going smoothly to allow myself to be distracted. After a while, my mother still hadn't appeared. I was getting increasingly nervous because I had to get to San Antonio for the game.

"What's going on?" I asked David when I called my mother's house. Days prior to my arrival, I asked him to tell her someone was honoring me with an award at an event being held at someone's house and I needed her to be there to accept it on my behalf.

"She's taking all day," he said. "She's trying to get the kinks out of that gold necklace of hers."

"I got to get out of here," I told him. "I just flew in for this and I got to go."

I had picked up two dozen red and white roses to present to her; I sat there with my roses, just waiting. I was so nervous, I was literally shaking. My girl Kim had come to Gulfport for the occasion.

She was there with me, but that didn't alleviate my nerves. Finally, I saw the car drive up. Both of my brothers were with her. I turned to the crowd and motioned for everybody to find a place to hide. Time felt like it was creeping ever so slowly as they made their way to the door.

When the doorbell rang, I took a deep breath, turned around, and opened the door. I tried to tell her what was happening, but right away when she saw me, she started screaming.

"Haaaaaa! Haaa!"

"Welcome home, Mama," I said.

I delicately grabbed hold of her and began walking her through the house. She was staring at everybody with a disbelieving look, as if she were in shock. I showed her the formal dining room, the kitchen, the bedrooms, the family room, the bookshelves (which even had a ladder that slid back and forth to reach the books on high shelves), the Jacuzzi out back, the garage, the walkways, the basketball court. Her bedroom was huge. When the tour was over, we greeted people and thanked them for coming. I walked her outside and turned to her.

"Mom, I just wanted to come back and present this to you," I said. "I love you. This is yours. This is not mine. God blessed me to get it. This is your house. You can even restrict me from being here if you choose."

But she wasn't fully understanding me.

"I got to get back home and clean up and—"

"Mom, this is your house," I said, interrupting her. "Any of that stuff you got back there? You can give it away."

"Well, I just got to go back," she said. "I have to go back home."

"Mama. This is your house."

I noticed Omar had an odd look on his face. He appeared to be sad. This was not going according to my plan.

"What's up with you?" I asked him.

He was still a child, just fourteen years old. So, he was still thinking like a child. He was upset because he didn't want to leave the neighborhood. He didn't want to leave Central Junior High.

"Look, man, don't worry about that," I said. "You won't have to switch schools, okay?"

Eventually he calmed down. I turned back to my mother, hoping it all was sinking in. I kissed her.

"I love you, Mom. But I have to get back. So I'm going to leave now."

I thanked everybody for coming. Kim and I then got into a car and headed to the airport. When I finally sat down on the plane to San Antonio, I felt a sense of calm that I hadn't felt in a long time. Even when the plane hit a stretch of turbulence, rather than my nerves twisting into a jumble, I still was able to relax.

God, if you take my life now, I'm good. I fulfilled a major goal. I got my mother the house of her dreams. I got her out of the ghetto. I'm good.

Tears felt heavy running down my face. Relief washed over me. I was happy.

CHAPTER 17

As I settled in and began to make a home in Denver, I found myself still searching for some greater meaning in my life. NBA basketball wasn't enough. I saw too much suffering around me, too much pain. I needed a more profound way to make sense of it all, to change the way I saw the world. The words of Malcolm X were still bouncing around in my head, making me question the inequities in American society — inequities I saw everywhere I turned. I wanted to be more like Malcolm, to understand more of what was being done to me and my people.

In Denver I befriended a good brother named Mark James, who worked at the Denver airport. Mark and I would spend hours sitting around talking about our lives, about the state of the world. One day Mark brought up Islam and said he was intrigued by the religion.

"Yeah, me too!" I said. "I read Malcolm and it's definitely been on my mind."

Mark told me he had met a Muslim brother at the airport who had advised him that he could go to a local masjid in Denver and pick up a Quran if he wanted to learn more about Islam. My eyes lit up. "Let's go!" I said.

The masjid was only about ten minutes from my home, down Evans Avenue. When we got there, we saw an Arab guy out front working on the lawn.

"Hey, brother, we were told that we can come here and get a Quran," I said to him. "We're interested in knowing more about Islam."

He studied us for a second. "Okay, come with me," he said.

He took us down to the basement, talking to us the whole time. I don't even remember what he said because I was so focused and excited about getting the Quran. I had never held one in my hands. The man gave us two copies of the book. We rushed back to my place, sat down at the breakfast table, and started reading our copies at the same time. I was only about two or three pages in when I began to feel overwhelmed by a sense of joy and assurance. The words were having a powerful effect on me. I looked up at Mark.

"I don't know about you, but my search is over," I said. "I'm going to be a Muslim. That's it for me."

He nodded. "Me too," he said.

We went back to reading. With each page, I felt more sure. There was no question in my mind. In those two to three pages, it's like all the questions I had were answered.

I went back to the masjid, a different one on Parker Road in another section of Denver. This time I was intent on transformation. I found an African American guy who was actually the janitor of the masjid. He became a teacher of sorts for me, answering my many questions every time I stopped by to talk to him. I kept reading the Quran and asking questions. By now my rookie season had ended. I went to a rookie review in Salt Lake City, like a tournament of NBA rookies. It wasn't mandatory but strongly encouraged. I read the Quran the whole time. When I got back to Denver in August, I immediately went to the masjid. I think Mark was with me. I walked in and announced to them that I wanted to embrace Islam. At that time, they gave me the Shahada, the Islamic declaration of faith. Recitation of the Shahada in Arabic is all that is required for a person to become a Muslim. In professing the Shahada, you are saying that you bear witness that there is nothing worth conforming to but Allah. He doesn't have partners; he doesn't have sons; he doesn't have daughters. You bear witness that Muhammad is His last prophet and messenger whom you seek to emulate. Since I came from a Christian background, it was similar to the baptism. After you recite the Shahada, if you've done it sincerely, all your sins are forgiven. You're like a newborn baby, fresh, without sin. It doesn't have to be done in front of an audience, but there should be at least two witnesses. I did it in front of an audience of Muslims in the masjid. Right after I was done, the imam brought me into his office. There was another brother in there with him.

"Have you chosen a name?" the imam asked me.

I shook my head. "No, I only know a few names. Like Muhammad Ali," I said, shrugging almost in apology for my ignorance.

"I think Mahmoud would be a good name for you," one of them said. The other one chimed in. "I think Abdul-Rauf would be a good name."

They both nodded at each other, satisfied with their selections.

The names sounded fine with me. They had excellent meanings: Mahmoud means "elegant" and "praiseworthy," and Abdul-Rauf means "servant of the beneficent or the kind." So I saw no problem.

"Okay," I said, nodding.

I've never been great with remembering names, but I've always been good with faces. As I started going to the masjid on a regular basis, I came to the realization that the imam and his partner had given me parts of their own names. After I got my hands on a book of Muslim names, I saw a bunch of names I would have rather had.

Awww, man! I wish I had this before! I thought. Suleman, which means "man of peace," would have been a great name. Or Mujahid, which means "striver of truth." *Oh, man, I'm a striver of truth! That's what I'm about! I could've been Mujahid.*

But it was too late; the community already knew me as Mahmoud Abdul-Rauf. I kept that name and eventually took the steps to make it legal.

The person who was most immediately affected by my reversion was Kim. We had gotten married at the end of my rookie NBA season. The wedding took place in a huge cathedral in New Orleans. I didn't believe in spending a whole lot of money on a wedding. I told her we could take the money and use it for something else, like helping out our families.

The marriage seemed like it ended before it had a chance to start. In retrospect I shouldn't have even gone through with it. I was becoming interested in Islam before the wedding took place. I could tell by her reaction to my interest that she wasn't happy. She was concerned, which is understandable.

One day I told her, "You know what? I'm thinking about being a Muslim."

"Why would you want to do that?" she said in a dismissive tone.

Instead of inquiring about what had led to my interest, showing any sort of curiosity about what was going on in my head, her immediate reaction sounded a lot like hostility. I should have put a halt on things at that point, but I went against my gut and married her anyway. When I look back, I think I was still fascinated by her beauty and body. There were other things that I should have noted as red flags. Even before I became Muslim, I've always liked women who are somewhat modest in their dress. Not to sound saintly, like my eyes don't gaze upon women who aren't modest, like I don't see that they're attractive. But we all have preferences, and what I'm looking to go home with is a woman who is not only modest in dress but, more important, modest in character. After all, who are you trying to impress? Kim didn't agree with that at all. That was another source of conflict. In addition, I thought she could be a little too materialistic. I didn't care for that. But these were things I decided to overlook. Being the competitive dude I am, I told myself, *If I'm the man I know I can be, she'll come around.* Clearly, that's an inexperienced and naive way to look at a relationship. If a person doesn't want to change, they won't change.

Once I embraced Islam, I would try to have conversations with her about certain things, but she deliberately rejected and ignored what I had to say. Naturally that led to conflict. My thinking was, *I'm not trying to force you to become something. I just want to share information with you, to see if your thinking can be influenced to look at something a different way. Maybe it will appeal to you.*

During that second year, Kim and I spent a lot of time apart. We would come together, have sex, talk a little bit. Then we'd separate again, and we wouldn't talk. One time she came to my place, and we were sitting there on the bed, talking. By that point we had already started discussing divorce. We didn't have children; we already spent most of our time apart. I gave her an "allowance," about $3,000, every two weeks, every time I got paid. Plus, I had bought her a Mercedes.

"Let me ask you a question," I said. "What do you think you need after we divorce?"

Without hesitation, she said, "A million dollars."

I was taken aback. I thought that was too much. I wasn't even making that much per year, after taxes. I told her she could keep the car and I would pay off her tuition, buy her a nice house, and put a comfortable amount of money in her account. But she wanted a million dollars.

"It's obvious you think you married a fool," I said. "If you're going to get that, you're going to have to get it through the courts."

That certainly ended all the talking on that night. But then I procrastinated and delayed serving her with divorce papers. I was told it looks better if you have them served. Eventually Kim ended up serving me. One day I got a knock on the door. I opened it and a guy handed me an envelope. Divorce papers.

When we settled out of court, I felt like I got railroaded. I truly thought my lawyer, a woman I hired, colluded with Kim's side and they tag-teamed me. I couldn't prove it; it was just a superstrong hunch. Kim won a settlement of $600,000. I didn't want to have to write her a check every month, so I just gave her a lump sum. *Take it, do what you want with it, you go your way and I go mine.* That was it. Over before it really started.

CHAPTER 18

On the Nuggets, for the first time in my life I had to get used to not being "the man," not being the focal point of the offense. I started just nineteen games my rookie season. There were seven guys who played more minutes than I did for the season. Point guard Michael Adams was our leading scorer, directing our run-and-shoot offense. Forward Orlando Woolridge and longtime All-Star Walter Davis were also scoring leaders for us.

With NBA rookies, they warn you to prepare to "hit the wall" midway through the season. In college, you might play close to forty games at the most, if you went far in the NCAA tournament. The NBA regular season is eighty-two games long, plus possibly many more if you make the playoffs. That means a rookie's body is going to notice when the season moves past the forty-game mark. Add on training camp and the preseason, plus traveling to forty-one away games in far-flung corners of the country—I discovered there was definitely some truth to the wall. I have to admit I checked out a little bit when we were halfway through that first season. Mentally, I just wasn't used to the grind yet. And did I mention the travel?

The casual NBA fan has no idea how much of an impact travel has on our bodies, our mindset, our lives. It was especially grueling my rookie year because we didn't have our own plane. We had to fly commercial, just like everybody else. We had to wake up early in the morning to fight through traffic and get to the airport on time. We had to wait in line to check in our bags, all the time not sure what kind of seat we were going to get. I'm not being an elitist here, but it all takes its toll. In the early 1990s, smoking was still permitted

on planes. If I was sitting next to a heavy smoker, I knew I would
spend the next couple of hours inhaling secondhand smoke. After we
landed, we had to go to baggage claim and wait. If somebody's bag
didn't show up, we all had to sit around and wait some more;
we couldn't leave until everybody's bag was accounted for. We
carried our bags to the bus and headed to the hotel. At the hotel
we waited for a room assignment, then brought our bags to our
room. Then we had to quickly turn around and head to the arena
for practice.

A few of the veterans usually got to fly in first class, but there
are only so many first-class seats on a plane. The rest of us were rel-
egated to coach, no matter how long our legs happened to be. When
Dikembe Mutombo joined the team my second season, he sat back in
coach with everybody else — all seven feet two inches of him. Needless
to say, Dikembe, who was the fourth pick in the draft, was not pleased.

After the game, my adrenaline was always sky-high. It was
like a sugar rush. When I returned to the room, no matter how late
it was, I wanted to get something to eat. By the time I actually got to
sleep, I might have only about ninety minutes or two hours before
I had to get up and head to the airport. If it was a 5:00 or 6:00 A.M.
flight, we had to be there at 3:00 or 4:00 in the morning. I never
seemed to get enough sleep. Sometimes I could sleep on the plane,
but not if I was sitting near a smoker.

When we played back-to-back — four games in five nights or
two games in three nights — it was especially tough. You had to figure
out how to stay focused. Man, that first year I couldn't wait for the
season to be over. Some teams had already figured out how much
better the team played when they had their own private plane. When
I found out the Detroit Pistons, who won back-to-back championships in 1989 and 1990, had their own plane, I thought, *No wonder
they keep winning!*

We got our own plane before my third season; I couldn't believe how much easier life on the road was. We won twelve more games that season than the previous year. The season after that we almost doubled our win total compared with two seasons before. The private plane took off from a private terminal, so we had our own parking spaces outside the terminal. We didn't have to fight through traffic to get there. We parked and brought our bags straight to the plane, dropped them there, and went up the steps to board. Inside, there were menus that catered to us, with a wide selection of food and beverages. There was fruit and snacks in the bins right above us, so we could eat what we wanted when we wanted. The seats were big and roomy, and no smoking was allowed. We could sleep peacefully from takeoff to touchdown. It was a world of difference.

After slimming down for my second season at LSU, I gained weight again before I reported to Denver, which certainly didn't help my cause with Coach Westhead. It was cluelessness that led to the weight gain. People kept telling me, "Hey, man, you got to be bulky before you go into the league!"

I had never worked with a trainer before; everything I did was me listening to my body and relying on my own ideas of what was going to work for me. At this stage of my career, listening to the wrong advice and not using reasoning proved to be costly. With that thought in my head—that I needed to be bigger—I went home and started eating. I had played my sophomore season at LSU at 169, but now I was getting comfortable with the idea of eating. I was working out, but it wasn't the same level of exercise I'd be doing in season. That means I was picking up weight the wrong way. I should have been putting on muscle; instead, I was putting on fat. When I reported to camp, my body fat was 19 percent, which was ridiculous. I damn near had a double chin. When I look back on my photos from that year, I can't believe how I look: the fat face, the obvious gut.

I convinced myself that everything was fine. When I got to training camp, I began to see that I had made a huge miscalculation. Playing with professionals who were in tip-top condition wasn't the same as playing with dudes in the neighborhood — dudes I could dominate. Right away I said to myself, *Uh-oh. This isn't good. I'm in terrible shape.*

Westhead already seemed like he didn't want me there; when he saw I was out of shape it made everything doubly worse. However, that doesn't excuse the way Westhead treated me. After all, I wasn't a troublemaker. I was obviously a good player, so clearly I had potential. Why wouldn't you conclude, *Okay, let's work with him and make our team better?* Of course, I was wrong for coming in out of shape. But I felt like I wasn't being handled properly when I got to Denver.

On top of my anguish over what was happening with the team, I also was trying to figure out how to be a grown man: pay bills, create a functioning household — you know, figure out where the power company is. And the weather wasn't helping. Cold. Real cold. Snow. This was not the winters of the Gulf Coast.

During games, Walter Davis often sat next to me on the bench. As I sat there tapping myself on the leg, the Tourette would start talking to me, telling me that to balance things out I also needed to tap Walter's leg. The first few times I did it, he looked at me, wondering what I wanted. I didn't look at him, but I could see him out of my peripheral vision. I didn't tell him that all I wanted was his leg to tap. With the Tourette, I was always in search of balance. Eventually, Walter got used to the tapping, no doubt thinking, *Oh, that's just something Mahmoud does. He taps my leg.*

When I was on the court, the TS often would bother me if I missed a shot or missed a pass. I knew I couldn't go back and do it again, but that doesn't mean it didn't bother me. When I missed a shot, I'd want to come down and hit a move and get back to that same shot. If the coach didn't give a particular direction and left it up to me, I was going to come back and try to do the same thing. A lot of times the game doesn't allow you to do that — it moves on and my defender may not give that to me — but my mind was still saying, *I got to do it again. I got to score.* It never leaves.

The fact that the team was losing all the time made the fans real ornery. They didn't care what I had done at LSU. What was I doing now? I was getting booed in my home gym. If I missed a couple of shots, the boos would rain down. This, I was not used to.

I learned that when NBA players aren't happy with their situation, it is their agent who does the complaining to management. I didn't think I could talk to Westhead anyway. We just never clicked. I found his personality to be strange, off-putting. I couldn't read his facial expressions. Sometimes when he smiled, it seemed fake to me. When he was gone, I found out he was a scholar of Shakespearean literature or something like that. Maybe he was thinking some high-level thoughts we weren't aware of, but he exuded a nervous energy, like he was jittery. For me, he was just difficult to be around.

I don't know if there was any kind of racial element to it. When you're African American, that's always a possibility, of course. Even when people are nice to you, you never actually know what they're thinking. They might be treating you a certain way totally out of self-interest, like, *This player is good for my career.* I just felt like it would be a waste of time for me to say anything to Westhead. I didn't think I would get an honest response from him.

Toward the end of my first season, I began to feel a pain in my ankles. I could still play and move, but it was nagging and didn't seem to be going away. Team doctors concluded that I had bone spurs, which would need to be removed. I didn't want the surgery, nor did I think I needed it. But when they offered it and said I would have to sit out the last few weeks of the season to recuperate, I jumped at it. At that point I was fighting depression, and I was looking for a way out of playing. This sounded like the perfect respite.

"Give me the surgery, man," I said.

I was bedridden, then in a wheelchair and using crutches for weeks. And I was eating, getting bigger and bigger, guaranteeing I would be even more out of shape when I came back for my second season. By the time I was ready to hit the court again, I was up to 192.

Even though my first season was a big disappointment for me, I did get selected to the NBA All-Rookie second team. But I wasn't impressed. I felt like my per game average of 14.1 points was deceptive, since my points mainly came during mop-up time, when we were losing and Westhead emptied the bench to give the starters a break.

The second season under Westhead wasn't much better for me. I began to perform better, but it felt like he was purposely playing games with me. He would put me in for little bursts, like four or five minutes at a time, but then yank me out. I thought he was trying to mess up my rhythm. It would have done no good to publicly complain about my treatment. In the minds of the fans, I was an athlete making millions; I just needed to shut up and dribble, no matter what private anguish I might be going through. That was the nature of the business.

At one point I decided I was not going to let Westhead mess with my head. I was getting all upset and letting him affect the way I did things, which I felt was giving him what he wanted. I could make three in a row, and he still would pull me from the game at odd times. If I pressed too much and missed, it would look better for him to take me out. I didn't have a very large window in which to make mistakes. I decided when he yanked me to always remain neutral. It took some of the pressure off. I would come in and hit on consecutive jumpers. *Pop. Pop. Pop.* When he took me out, I would walk off with a neutral facial expression, neutral body language. Let nobody see that I was upset. I would silently say a prayer: *Please, God, bless me to be patient. Bless me to be humble. Bless me to be strong. Bless me to stay focused. Bless me to stay balanced.*

I would sit down, still keeping my expression as neutral as possible. I've never been the cheerleader type, so I wouldn't say much as I sat on the bench. I told myself that Westhead clearly was going to get rid of me as soon as he had the chance. So, I should stop worrying about it and just do me. When I made that mental change, I noticed that external things began to change. I started playing better—and fans started booing Westhead when he took me out. They even began to chant, "Put Rauf in! Put Rauf in!"

I would deliberately try to block the fans out, staying neutral so I wouldn't encourage it or feed it in any way. I knew that it could easily turn against me in an instant. People are fickle like that. I was still battling with my weight, but I had some help come in an unexpected way. Since I had accepted Islam the summer before, I celebrated my first Ramadan in March. Ramadan is the monthlong Muslim devotional commemorating Prophet Muhammad's revelation of the Quran. During Ramadan, Muslims must fast every day without eating, drinking, or engaging in sexual activity from sunrise to nightfall. Through fasting, I lost almost 20 pounds, getting down close to 170. I could feel the difference on the court. However, Westhead remained unmoved.

His attitude toward me was perfectly exemplified during the last game of the season. My mother had flown into Denver for the game, the first time I believe she had come to see me play in the NBA. She sat with the players' wives and families; I introduced her to my teammates and Nuggets management. People made sure she felt welcomed and special. Everybody except for Westhead. He knew my mother was there, but he didn't play me at all the entire game. In the last two minutes of the game, Westhead got down on one knee and gazed at the bench. I looked out at the court and pretended I wasn't watching him, though I could see him with my peripheral vision. Westhead knew he was wrong. I could sense that. I'd dropped weight; I was showing signs of what I used to be. So why wouldn't you play me — unless you were trying to mess with my head?

I could see him looking at me, then looking at the player who was sitting next to me — I can't remember who that was. He kept looking back and forth between us, as if he was considering whether he was going to put me through this final indignity, making me sit the entire game with my mom watching. With his eyes on me, he called out the other player's name and told him to go in. He was still looking at me, surely waiting for my response.

I chuckled softly. Without looking at him, still watching the action on the court, I spoke — not loud, but enough for him to hear: "That's okay. Have your laugh now. But just know one thing: God willing, I'll be here long after you're gone."

Shortly after that game, Westhead was fired. He had taken over a winning team that had been in the playoffs the previous year, and in two seasons, his record was 44–120. I had called it: I stayed in Denver; he didn't.

CHAPTER 19

By the end of my second season, I was struggling with depression so acute that I began to think about quitting. I wasn't happy at all. Playing in the NBA was not what I imagined it would be, especially considering my situation in Denver. I was questioning myself, fighting self-doubt. I looked at my finances and asked myself, *Can I take the contract I have now and figure out how to make enough money from it so that I don't have to play anymore?*

I was looking real hard for an exit route, wondering whether this was something I still wanted. Back then, there wasn't any room in the public sphere for a professional athlete to admit he was battling mental health issues. When Kendall Gill, the guard out of the University of Illinois who was the fifth pick in my draft class, spoke out publicly about battling mental health challenges, I recall hearing people grumbling that he was just making excuses. The public just didn't want to hear about anything that might prevent us from going out there on the court and performing for their benefit. Our job was to entertain; we were not to let anything get in the way of that. Even injuries. We were supposed to fight through the pain, to suck it up. If that was the public stance on physical injuries, I knew there was no chance that I would get anything but attacked if I talked about my mental health. It's more accepted now; the public is much more accustomed to thinking about the importance of mental health.

I tried to use prayer as a path out of my depression. It was a habit passed down from my grandmother, and my aunt and uncle, that I could pray to a higher power to help with my troubles. *God, help me. I'm miserable.*

It never got to the point of suicidal ideation or anything, but I was talking through these issues in my head, saying I didn't want to live like this anymore, dealing with all the drama. Then one night before the start of my third season, I had an experience that proved to be transformative. I was in a Denver grocery store picking up some stuff, accompanied by my childhood friend Shaheed Ali, who was visiting from Gulfport. We were walking down the magazine aisle when a cover headline about the NBA caught my eye. I stood there quickly thumbing through it. When I saw my picture, I read through the accompanying story and was stunned. The article called me a "bust." It was like a sword had been plunged into my belly. I felt a literal pain when I saw that word associated with me. With all the problems I was dealing with in Denver, it was a wake-up call to realize how I was being perceived by the outside world. I was seen as a failure. Standing in that aisle, in that moment I made the decision that I would commit myself to transformation. As I put the magazine back in the rack, I was a changed man.

I devised a regimen I stayed with the entire summer. I woke up in the morning and drove to the Cherry Creek Sporting Club in Denver. I did the StairMaster for an hour at the highest intensity. I flew in guys to play one-on-one for hours at a time—guys like my Gulfport partner Leonard Bennett, who had played college at New Orleans, and Francisco "Boo" Hardy, who played at Mississippi Valley State. I would give them car keys and tell them to meet me at the gym, where we would do two-a-days. I told myself I had worked too hard to get to the NBA to squander it, to be in a position where somebody could call me a bust. In addition to the workouts, I changed my diet. I ate a lot of salads and seafood and basically cut out fried foods. I went back to my youth, when I would use motivation like the deprivation in my family and my community to piss me off and make me work so hard I felt like I was going to die. I realized

I had gotten too comfortable; I had gotten away from the work ethic that got me to the NBA in the first place. It was a classic dilemma: you work for something your whole life, but what happens when you actually get it and realize it's not what you expected?

After several months of hard work, I began to feel differently. I went through the stages of change. First you feel different, before you actually see any changes. Usually what happens next is somebody sees it before you do. People started telling me, "Man, you look good!" What that does is build confidence, makes you push yourself even harder—even if you don't see any difference yet in the mirror. The last step is for you to actually see the difference. I see these same stages now when I train players.

When time came for me to report to training camp, I weighed about 155 pounds—down from about 190 at my heaviest. I hadn't been that light since high school.

My outside affirmation came in the form of the coach who was hired to replace Paul Westhead, the former Nuggets star Dan Issel. Issel had retired from the Nuggets as a player after the 1985 season and did the Nuggets television broadcasts from 1988 to 1992. When he retired, he was the Nuggets's all-time leading scorer and was fourth on the league's all-time combined ABA/NBA scoring list after Kareem Abdul-Jabbar, Wilt Chamberlain, and my idol, Julius Erving. Issel, who was inducted into the NBA Hall of Fame in 1993, came to us with serious basketball credentials, a man who had played at the highest level.

During training camp, Issel did an interview in which he said that when he got the job, I was one of the first people he met with. He told me that what happened in the past with the team would stay in the past; he was looking forward to me being a major contributor. He also said during the interview that I had come into training camp looking like a different player, one who was now in excellent shape.

He said that he disagreed with all the talk saying I wasn't a good defender. "He can play defense," Issel said.

The weight loss and training paid immediate dividends for me. I found that I could get to my spots on the floor easier. I had always enjoyed when players underestimated my strength because of my relatively small frame. But they would find out when they tried to post me up that I was stronger than I looked. This was even truer after I slimmed down. I knew how to stay low to get better leverage, which made it harder to move me. I saw right away that my speed had picked up. The game had become easier for me. A lot of this was because of my improved stamina. If you have two players who are equal in skill level and athleticism, but one is in better shape, by the third or fourth quarter, the one with more stamina is going to start looking a whole lot better. Not because he is, but because his conditioning didn't fail him. Conditioning and focus go hand in hand; once you get tired, your focus flies out the window. Your technique crumbles. Instead of wanting the ball to attack, when you get the ball, you're trying to find somebody else to pass it to. When I was in tip-top shape, I found that I could stay focused much longer. My moves stayed tight and crisp throughout the game. It became clearer to me that what hurt me most the first two seasons was being out of shape. I couldn't get to the spots I wanted on the floor.

I started every game that season. I finished with an average of 19.2 points per game, which led the team. My 4.2 assists per game was second on the team to Robert Pack, who averaged 4.4 assists. I made 217 out of 232 free throws to finish with a .935 percentage, which was second in the NBA to Mark Price's .948 free throw percentage. The team finished with a record of 36–46, which wasn't great but was a twelve-win improvement over the previous season.

My dramatically improved performance was noticed around the league, and I won the NBA's Most Improved Player award.

Though I'm not one to prioritize those types of awards, that one did feel good when I thought back on that magazine article that sparked the turnaround. Maybe not a bust after all, huh?

I had an unexpected offer come along during the NBA All-Star break. I didn't make the All-Star team, but I did get invited to participate in the slam dunk contest, even though I had never dunked in an NBA game. I'm not sure who put my name in the hat—it surely wasn't me. What happened was, after I got in shape, I started dunking a lot in practice. Before and after practice, I would have dunk contests with Robert Pack, a 6'2" guard from USC who dunked all the time in games. The other guys would watch us go at each other in dunk-offs. Guys started telling me I should be in the NBA dunk contest, in addition to the three-point shooting contest. Somebody tipped off the NBA, and we got word that the league wanted me to participate.

My initial reaction was that I didn't want to go. Even though being selected to participate in the popular contest during All-Star weekend was a very nice honor, I much preferred using those three days to visit with family and decompress from the long slog of the NBA season. I also found that I treasured the chance to get away from the business of the NBA. I loved my teammates, but getting away from the team politics and intrigue was priceless. I looked forward to hearing the laughter and conversation of regular folk, to go eat, relax, read, and enjoy not having a set schedule to dictate my actions.

Because of my ambivalence, I traveled to Salt Lake City with my heart not fully invested. I had just resumed dunking that summer; dunking requires rhythm and timing, which I hadn't yet fully recaptured. My strategy was all wrong, too. I expended too much energy dunking during the warm-ups. I should have paced myself better. When the contest started, I wasn't jumping as high as

I normally would, which reduced the wow factor of the dunks I did. If you go to YouTube, you can watch my inadequate efforts. Right before my first dunk, you can hear the commentators mention how much weight I had lost. That might have been the highlight for me. High-flying Harold Miner won that year—his first of two wins, the second coming two years later in 1995.

Probably the craziest aspect of my participation in the contest is that I never dunked in an NBA game. Not even once during my entire career, before and after the dunk contest. Clearly, I was able, but it was a strategic decision on my part. The NBA season is eighty-two games long—many months of serious exertion and bodily wear and tear. When I looked at the guards who did a lot of dunking in games, I saw that many of them ended up having knee injuries. We already do a lot of cutting, jumping, and landing, without factoring in the dunks. Especially for guards who are relatively short, like me, repeatedly rising up to the basket with the kind of force you need to dunk and then landing properly puts significant stress on your knees and ankles. The risk of landing awkwardly or on the side of some guy's foot is dramatically increased during dunks. If you watch a lot of basketball, you often see guys get hurt when they land awkwardly after taking off. By my calculation, if I'm driving on you and I have the advantage, with you hustling to cut me off, I'm usually going to choose to stop and pop. Why? It's less of a distance to travel. If I'm in the lane and it's open, I'm going to take the layup. But if I get to the lane and see somebody there, I'm going to take the jump shot. I felt just as comfortable making my jump shot as I did making a layup. In my mind, the probability of success was just as high. Therefore, I would choose the easier road, the less risky road, and preserve my body.

I led the team in scoring every year, averaging 18 points in 1993–94, 16 points in 1994–95, and 19.2 points in 1995–96, but that was often from creating my own shots. Considering how many minutes I played, I tended to have far fewer free throw attempts than many of my teammates. But when I stepped up to the line, I converted. In the four seasons from 1992 to 1996, I led the NBA in free throw shooting two times (1993–94 and 1995–96) and finished second in 1992–93 and seventh in 1994–95. In 1993–94, when I led the league with a percentage of .956, I missed only 10 free throws out of 229 attempts the entire season. The .956 remains the third-highest season percentage in NBA history (after Jose Calderon's 98.1 percent in 2008–2009 and Calvin Murphy's 95.8 percent in 1980–81).

After I began finding success, leading the team in scoring during consecutive seasons, I would have expected to have the offense built around my skills. But that never happened. I was never the focal point of the team's offense. I was never given the carte blanche green light to shoot that I had in college or that my NBA contemporaries like Allen Iverson and Isiah Thomas had on their teams.

In Denver, our offense was built around the big man in the middle, Dikembe Mutombo, even though Dikembe was never an offensive-minded player. Dikembe earned his keep—he was always the team's highest-paid player—blocking shots and snatching rebounds. Nevertheless, our number one goal when we came down was to throw it in to the big man. The coaches were trying to establish him as the team's go-to.

I love Dikembe, but I just didn't think he should have been the offensive go-to guy. It would bother me at times that I was never seen as "the guy." My thinking was, *Dang, what's a brother gotta do?* I took it personal, but in a good way, as fuel to push me even harder. I decided that I wasn't going to complain; I would just go out there and do my thing and let the chips fall. *It's gonna be what it's gonna be.* They knew what my skills were—what good was complaining going to do anyway? I told myself, *Stay humble, Mahmoud. Stay hungry. God willing, things will work themselves out.*

Under Issel, we made the playoffs in 1993–94 with a record of 42–40. We were the eighth seed, but we managed to beat the top-seeded Seattle SuperSonics 3–2 in a five-game series — the first time in league history an eighth seed had beaten a top seed in the playoffs. We lost to the Utah Jazz in the next round after pushing them to a seventh game. We made the playoffs again the following year with a record of 41–41, but got swept by the San Antonio Spurs, led by Sean Elliott and David Robinson, in the opening round.

Midway through the 1994–95 season, there was chatter around me that I was going to make the All-Star team. I'm not sure where it first came from, perhaps someone in the front office. The day before the fan voting was to be closed, I was told that I was the leading vote getter among guards in the West. Back then, the fans picked the starters, and the head coaches in each conference picked the reserves. I went to bed that night believing I was likely going to be on the team. I was having a pretty good season up to that point, and we were winning more than we were losing.

The next day when the squads were announced, I wasn't even on the team. I was perplexed; how did I go from being the leading vote getter to not even being on the squad? All I could do was chuckle.

I had recently officially changed my NBA name to Abdul-Rauf — it was now on my jerseys and everything else. It felt like somebody had it in for me. Even though I didn't want to travel to the game and give up those days off, I thought the whole episode was odd. But how would it look if I publicly spoke out and asked questions? I would look stupid and delusional. I had no evidence of any kind, just my suspicions. I decided to just let it be.

CHAPTER 20

One day during Friday prayer at the masjid in Denver, the imam talked about Hajj, the pilgrimage to Mecca, telling us that anyone with the means to go was obligated to make the trip to Saudi Arabia. One of the five pillars of Islam, Hajj is a religious duty that all adult Muslims are mandated to carry out at least once in their lifetimes if they are physically, mentally, and financially capable of making the journey.

I certainly had the means; I began to figure out when I would be able to go. Because the Islamic calendar is lunar and the Islamic year is about eleven days shorter than the Gregorian year (which most of the world uses), the Gregorian date for Hajj changes from year to year, starting ten or eleven days earlier each year. When I looked into it, I saw that I needed to do it in May 1993. The next year we would still be in the NBA season when it occurred—and each successive year after that for many years.

I had read about Hajj for the first time in Malcolm X's autobiography, but I hadn't studied it in depth. At the time, I still wasn't acclimated to a steady diet of reading and studying, like I am now. I got a lot of tips and cautions in the days leading up to the trip. One brother told me that when you go to Hajj, all your sins are forgiven. Your slate is wiped clean, like a newborn baby. But your mindset had to be right when you were there; otherwise your Hajj would be disrupted, invalidated. I was told if I lost my patience with people, it could invalidate my Hajj. At the time I heard it, I didn't realize just how much of a challenge that warning would pose.

I didn't want to go by myself, so I brought two brothers with me: Bashir, who owned Salaam Books, and Muhammad Sharif, who had already been numerous times. It was a huge help to me having Sharif along to guide me during my first visit. Since I had the means, I considered it my duty to be a blessing to others and pay for them to make the pilgrimage.

The plane to Mecca was filled with Muslim pilgrims. During the flight, at times various people would take the mic and begin to pray out loud. It was an amazing feeling, to be on this journey with all these people, strangers to me but my brothers and sisters in faith.

After we landed, it didn't take long for my patience to be tested. I was accustomed to a certain American protocol concerning waiting in line. Over here, we know someone is asking for trouble if they cut in front of others in line. Somebody is gonna speak up: "Hey, man, what are you doing? You got to get to the back of the line!"

Not so in Saudi Arabia during Hajj. People were constantly getting in front of me, pushing their way to the front of the lines. I kept taking deep breaths and reminding myself: *Don't lose your patience. Don't lose your patience. Don't lose your patience.* I would pray and breathe, pray and breathe. My Tourette, which is exacerbated by extra agitation, nervousness, or anger, was constantly on the verge of exploding. I had to keep talking and praying to myself to keep everything under control.

The inside of the airport was a breathtaking spectacle: enormous crowds of pilgrims filled with anticipation as we all headed to the same place. Not being able to speak the language, I was constantly watching others to figure out what I was supposed to be doing. We were all heading toward the Kaaba, the most sacred site in all of Islam. The Kaaba, a building at the center of Islam's most important masjid, al-Masjid al-Haram, represents the metaphorical house of God. All Muslims around the world face toward the Kaaba during our five daily prayers.

On the way to the Kaaba, we had to enter the state of ihram, which required going through a cleansing ritual and putting on the ihram clothing: a two-piece unstitched white garment intended to make everyone appear the same. The sameness signifies that in front of God there is no difference among us, no matter your riches or station in life. As we move toward the Kaaba, we are all unified in appearance and purpose, brothers and sisters joining together to conform to Allah.

I met so many wonderful, fascinating people on the way to the Kaaba. I met an African brother from Sudan who was incredibly striking in appearance—his white clothing looked flawless, without wrinkles, even though he was sitting down, and he had the whitest teeth and the most beautiful unblemished skin I had ever seen in my life. He exuded an angelic aura, with bright, knowing eyes and soft flowing hair. When he spoke, he sounded like a very learned, intellectually acute man. Meeting these people and having stimulating conversations opened my eyes and filled me with a passionate desire to travel the world, to learn as much as I could about all the mesmerizing people who inhabit this planet.

At the Kaaba, where we all circumambulated the building in the center, we were pressed together so tightly, shoulder to shoulder, ankle to ankle, I gave in to the movement of the crowd and just went with the flow. People were pushing and throwing elbows, but I ignored it all, breathing and praying and not resisting.

When I was in Saudi Arabia, I already had an awareness of the Saudi leadership's historical animus toward Islam. It was a government run as a dictatorship, by a family that had the arrogance to name the country after themselves and to treat the Arabian Peninsula and its natural material, including mineral resources, and Mecca as their personal and private property—disregarding the fact that this wealth belongs to and should be used for the Muslims. A family who restricts the number of Muslims allowed to make Hajj every year to around two million over the course of two weeks, when Hajj is actually three months long and could accommodate millions more. And then they herd us in and out as quick as cattle. The abuses are great and grave. During Hajj, we are obligated to publicly denounce imperialism, sectarianism, oppression of all kinds — yet the Saudis are guilty of them all.

When I returned home, I felt reinvigorated and committed to doing even more reading, more learning. I talked to many people in the Muslim community to soak up more information and to find the authors I should be reading. I was on a journey of self-enlightenment, reconditioning my mind to become a much more studious person than I had ever been. It was a significant lifestyle change for me. I was seriously motivated to transform myself. Of course, it's a process, and there were days when I was less committed than I wanted to be — it wasn't all study all the time.

I also began the process of formally changing my name. I didn't want to do it before I left the country. I had never traveled abroad before; I was nervous about the complications it might cause if I suddenly had a new name on my passport. When the judge asked me the reason for the name change, I told him it was for religious reasons. But it was more than that. The act of naming something or someone is a powerful act, especially knowing the history of our ancestors brought to America. As the activist Randall Robinson said, "I know of no other example in the modern world where millions of people from a single racial group had been stripped of everything save respiratory function — mother, father, child, property, language, culture, religion, freedom, dignity, and, sometimes, even genitalia. Now he is a menace to society." I aimed to take ownership by accepting a name for myself and taking away this sense of white property ownership that comes with accepting a name that reeks of slavery. But conveying this to a white judge would have certainly delayed the process, so I judiciously kept it to myself.

I wasn't sure how the folks back in Gulfport would react to the name change, and I didn't care, but I was pleased by my mother's reaction. Eventually, at least. I did have a few shaky moments with her at first. The first time I told her about the change, she said, "Oh, baby, that's good. Everybody needs something to believe in. That's all right."

Literally the very next day I called her and, in response to something she said, I reminded her, "Mom, you know I'm a Muslim, right?"

"Who you been listening to, boy? Who's convincing you? You don't have a mind —"

"Whoa, whoa, whoa," I said.

My mother and I talked often, and she'd known since I was young that once my mind is made up about something, it's made up.

"Mom, I love you, but let me make this clear," I continued. "This is what I believe. You're my mother, I love you, but you can do whatever — you can disown me, you can not want to have anything to do with me. But God wills, I will not abandon the idea and the belief of being a Muslim for nobody. I love you with everything in me, but this is what I've decided for myself, and this is what I'm going to be, whether you like it or not."

My mother never again questioned my relationship with Islam after that conversation. Knowing me, she knew I wouldn't bend or waver. I would sit with her sometimes and have exchanges with her about the ideology of Islam and the many principles it shared with Christianity: commitment to charity; belief in the afterlife, in angels, in the Bible/Quran, in destiny and fate — all of these beautiful concepts. Belief in the power of being neighborly, not just in the local sense but also globally. She never embraced Islam, but I think she grew to respect it. And she definitely noticed the change in me, and she liked it — although I was never one of those children who gave my mother a lot of problems anyway.

Soon after our initial conversations, I was with her in Gulfport when somebody called out to me, "Hey, Chris!"

She turned and quickly said, "No. That's not his name no more. His name is Mahmoud."

I smiled to myself, pleased to hear her come to my defense. It was a big moment for us.

As I expected, not everybody in Gulfport chose to respect my beliefs. People would purposely call me Chris instead of Mahmoud. As a matter of fact, that still happens, even though I've now been a Muslim longer than I was a Christian and Mahmoud Abdul-Rauf longer than I was Chris Jackson. Usually it's a very old person who still chooses to call me Chris. Sometimes I let it go, but sometimes I'll push back:

"Well, you know, Miss Such-and-Such, my name is Mahmoud."

"Oh. Well, baby, you know that's hard for me to say."

"You know what? That's okay," I'll say. "No problem. You call me what you want."

But all the time I'm thinking, *You can't say my name? Two syllables. Mah-moud. Like you in a good mood. Not that difficult. But you can say names like Arnold Schwarzenegger? Schwarzenegger! Four syllables!*

I realized it wasn't that these people had a problem pronouncing it; they just didn't want to try. Some people were even arrogant about their refusal. One afternoon, I dropped off a friend of mine at this middle-aged lady's house. I don't remember what he was there for. While I waited for him in the driveway, the lady talked to me from behind her screen door while I sat at the wheel. Mind you, I couldn't even see her, but I could hear her. She kept on referring to me as Chris. Chris this, Chris that. On and on she went. She said my old name so many times, I became convinced that she was purposely trying to push my buttons.

"My name is Mahmoud now," I told her.

"Well, Chris, your mama named you Chris so that's what I'm going to call you."

Now she was arrogantly advertising her ignorance, which provoked me. "My mama don't have anything to do with this," I said, trying to keep my voice from rising. "Listen here. As a grown man I can divorce myself from whatever name given to me to choose one significant to how I see myself. And I would expect that you would show some decency and acknowledge my wishes."

"Well, you'll always be Chris to me," she said defiantly.

"Now listen. We don't have anything else to talk about. If you can't respect the fact that I chose a name for myself, then stop talking to me."

But she wouldn't back down.

"Well, you know, *Chris*—"

"Okay, Mumbawala," I said. I was so mad, I made up an outlandish name for her on the spot, the first thing that came into my head.

"That ain't my name!" she said.

"That's who you gonna be from here on out. If you keep calling me out my name, I'm gonna call you out your name!"

We went back and forth a few more times, while I'm wondering where in the world my boy is so I can get away from this ridiculous woman. But then I remembered the verse in the Quran where Allah says when you're confronted with a person who is ignorant, and they are arrogant with their ignorance, just say, "Peace," and leave them alone. That's what I did.

"Okay, ma'am. Peace to you," I said. Then I rolled up the window and waited in silence.

Inside the Nuggets organization, initially no one seemed to have a problem with my reversion. They changed the name on my jersey without any pushback. They saw how serious I was. I wasn't disrespectful or arrogant and always tried to carry myself with humility but also strength, so there was no valid reason for anybody to be alarmed. I wasn't going out to clubs or drinking alcohol or doing drugs; why should they be concerned? No big deal, right? That seemed to be their position at first. After all, this is a country where so many people's religious convictions were handed down to them, beliefs that were not very deep or layered because most people had never had them challenged or been forced to think about them intensely. Here was a guy who had been purposeful with his choice.

When I encountered Muslims as I went about my daily business, they often would express surprise over my religion. A guy picked me up to bring me to the airport, and when I saw his name, Mansour, I asked if he was Muslim. He said he was, so I gave him the universal greeting, "As-salamu alaykum," which means "peace be upon you" in Arabic. He responded, "Wa-alaykumu s-salamu," which translates to "may peace be upon you." But as we rode, he felt compelled to ask me some pointed questions.

"Where are you from?"

It was a question I often get from Muslims. What they assume is, if you are Muslim, you must be from another country. "I'm from here. The United States," I said.

"No, no, no. Where are your people from?"

I shrugged. "Many of us African Americans don't know where we're from. Because of the history of slavery, a lot of our people being raped, I don't know exactly where I came from. But I was born in this country, in Mississippi."

He frowned. Muslims see America as a corrupt, hypocritical country, with a ruthless, unprincipled military — it's often called the "belly of the beast." Reconciling native-born Americans with the principles of Islam is hard for many to grasp.

"Man, you are better than me," he said.

"Why do you say that?"

He paused. "Well, I was born Muslim. This is all I know. You had to go through the process of thinking about it, of processing it, analyzing it. And you changed something and became something else. I grew up in it."

I thought about what he said and nodded. He was right. I had definitely done plenty of processing and analyzing.

Over time, I saw the tacit acceptance inside the Nuggets organization begin to change. I could tell that I was making people uncomfortable. They would see me praying every day, reading all these heavy books, engaging in provocative conversations with people on the plane or the bus. When we arrived in different cities, I often went off with various Muslim brothers. In the team's eyes, there's Mahmoud going off again with these people who are dressed funny, going up to visit him in his room. While teammates were using their downtime to do different things and occasionally go out to clubs and the like, I rejected all of that. They never saw me drinking or smoking or partying. Those things didn't interest me.

It was never my intent to be provocative, but my curiosity about the world was exploding. I wanted to know stuff. I wanted to know what people thought about things. After all those years of indifference, I was like a man who didn't know he was dying of thirst coming upon a water hole for the first time. I wanted to drown in knowledge. I felt like I had deprived myself. I began to feel cheated because I discovered so much I had been taught, so much that I thought I knew about the world, about the country, about politics and history and economics, wasn't entirely true. I was angry about it. I began to imagine how much more self-confidence and self-esteem I would have had growing up if I had been given access to this information about Black people, about the glorious past of kingdoms in Africa. Who knows—I might not have even become a basketball player.

I would read one book and I would come across references to other books. I would go get those and see references to still others. It was like a trail of crumbs leading me to enlightenment. Once I got the information, I wanted to share it with as many people as I could. I was a man who had been intellectually reborn.

But that's when I became a problem for the Nuggets. One of the first points of conflict to arise was over my praying before games. I would usually go to the equipment room to pray. It was located right off the locker room, not far from everyone else, but it afforded me some privacy to lay down my prayer rug. If they had started the pregame meeting before I was done, I'd catch up and find out what I missed. I knew the plays; not much was going to change from game to game. After the game, I would go to the same spot and pray again. I consider myself a people person, but during these times I preferred to sit and be reflective, not engaging in a lot of banter with teammates.

Dan Issel revealed during a recent interview that management didn't understand what I was doing. But in my mind, as long as I was acting in a professional manner, taking care of my business on and off the court, it shouldn't have mattered to them what I was doing. I wasn't in violation of team rules. I wasn't in the clubs; I wasn't getting drunk or high; I wasn't late for practice; I was staying in shape. He said management would wonder what I was doing with the Muslims who would come up to my room and talk to me late into the night. He wondered, *What are they talking about?*

I felt like they were concerned about the wrong things. They should have been focusing on the guys who were wearing themselves out before the game with the partying. I was just trying to get enlightened, sleeping and praying and playing, and I'm the problem?

It made no sense to me. But I knew if I wasn't acting like one of the boys, like part of the country club, people were going to look at me with some sort of side-eye. I was the pious dude seeing the guys who were married meeting other women on the road. I'm sure that didn't always sit well with those guys, almost like I had some moral superiority that was making everyone uncomfortable.

At times, I would purposely be antagonistic just to see how the coaching staff would react. We would be on the plane or the bus, where the coaches sat in the front and we sat behind them. They were cool as long as guys were sleeping, listening to music, playing dominoes or cards, or gossiping about something. But if I asked a question about a controversial subject, like politics or socioeconomics, I could see them get upset. I would deliberately throw out a provocative statement to my teammates and watch the coaching staff from behind, as they shook their heads back and forth in their seats. As if they were saying, "Here we go again!" That's when I knew my presence was a problem for them.

One day an assistant coach named Mike Evans, an African American guy who had played in the NBA for several teams, including the Nuggets, approached me. He told me that Nuggets staff had been watching how I was practicing Islam and praying before the games. He said Issel was concerned that I was missing part of the meetings.

"You know, I talked to a Muslim scholar, and he told me that, um, you don't have to pray before the games," he said.

The team was in a losing skid at the time, and I think they were looking to pass around blame. Players showing up late to meetings always sounded like a good excuse. I think there was also some condescension involved: *Oh, he's just an athlete; he's probably not done any reading or research, he's just doing what somebody told him to do. So, let's hit him with "scholar" and shut this praying thing down real quick.*

I looked at Evans and chuckled. "Mike, if you want to know anything about Islam, don't go behind my back trying to see if I'm practicing my religion right," I said. "If anything, you need to focus on the practice of your own religion." I shook my head. "Number two, that's correct and also incorrect. Can I wait? Yeah. But in the Quran, Allah says clearly that you pray when it's time. But if you sense danger, if you're in a dangerous situation, you remember Allah while standing, sitting, and on your side. And when that danger no longer is present, you resume praying as you have been instructed."

I looked around the locker room in an exaggerated fashion.

"The last time I checked, I didn't see any type of imminent danger or war zone in this gym, where I would have to be forced to delay my prayer."

He stared at me without responding.

"Mike, in the future, if you got something to ask me, you can come ask me. If I don't know the answer, I'll find it for you. You don't have to go behind my back trying to see if I'm practicing my religion correctly, 'cause it's an insult."

To his credit, a day or so later Mike approached me again. "Man, I apologize," he said. "You were correct. I should've come to you."

"Fair enough. I appreciate it," I said. I respected him for coming back to me with an apology. But the fact that he had approached me in the first place gave me a window into the reaction management was having to my religious transformation.

At the time I was reading a lot of books and articles that were making me more attuned to the political hypocrisies of the United States. The Quran says we must speak out against injustice, even if it's against our own selves. A few years later, I came across a statement by Arundhati Roy, the Indian activist and writer, that perfectly summarized my beliefs: "The trouble is that once you see it, you can't unsee it. And once you've seen it, keeping quiet, saying nothing, becomes as political an act as speaking out. There's no innocence. Either way, you're accountable."

Allah tells us to not be like a donkey carrying books — don't have all this knowledge and not put it to use. As I read more, the people I admired began to change. No longer were they athletes like Dr. J (no offense to the contributions athletes make); now I was admiring people who took strong positions: Fannie Lou Hamer, Ida B. Wells, Harriet Tubman, Malcolm X, Marcus Garvey, Patrice Lumumba, MLK, Nat Turner, Denmark Vesey, Gabriel Prosser. These people became my influences. In my free time, I was no longer sitting in front of a television watching basketball or mindless movies. I was reading books and having my mind blown. *Oh my goodness!* I would say to myself when I came across a particularly powerful passage. *Did you see how he put that together?*

Learning about this stuff was making me über-excited — and also extremely angry. Amos Wilson's *The Developmental Psychology of the Black Child* had a profound impact on me. He talked about how most of what children should learn should be introduced before they're seven years old to mold and shape them. I read about how the State Department funded a Harvard study showing how African children excel at an early age compared with European children in a wide range of categories, from their intellectual capacity to hand-eye coordination, but the advantages disappear once they are subjected to Western schools. My eyes were opened to all the doors that remain closed for Black people in American society, a system set up for us to fail. That was the road I was on — a road that was far from the one professional sports leagues prefer their players to be walking.

W hen I played for Gulfport High, there were two sisters, the Dotson girls, who came to all our games, sometimes with their mother. They went to a local private school, St. John, but the family was big fans of Gulfport High. Vicky was older than April, but I didn't pay that much attention to either of them because they were both younger than me. After I got to the league, I returned home to attend a benefit game. I didn't play in it; I was just a spectator.

At one point during the game, I saw a beautiful young woman in the bleachers as I passed by. I noticed right away that it was April Dotson. Several years had passed since I had last seen her, and from what I was seeing, those years had been very good to her. While I was gone, little April had grown into a stunning woman. Her caramel skin had a glow to it, like she was perpetually followed around by a beam of the golden sunlight that appears just before dusk. She was wearing a pair of cutoff shorts, what we called "Daisy Dukes" at the time, named after that white woman on *The Dukes of Hazzard* TV show. Her legs were incredible. The whole effect was breathtaking. I couldn't believe it was April.

I was in the midst of my divorce from Kim; I had no plans to go over and talk to her. But she took care of that herself. Van Gross, an ex-teammate at Gulfport High, came over to me.

"Hey, man," he said. "April wants to say hello."

"Okay."

I went over and talked to her briefly. She was all smiles and sweetness. But I didn't prolong it too much. I went back to my seat. After the game, Van came back over. He told me he was dating her sister, Vicky.

"Hey, I'm going over to their house. You should come with me. April likes you. She wouldn't mind."

I was intrigued, so I told him I would meet him there. I drove over to their house; I went inside and spoke to their mother. I had met their mom before but had never talked to her at length. It didn't take long for somebody to look out the window at my car, a sleek black Mercedes convertible with gray trim. April and I went outside so she could see it up close.

"Do you want to drive it?" I asked.

"What?" She sounded amazed and nervous at the same time.

"It's fine," I said.

She slid behind the wheel, and we went on a little expedition. She was enjoying herself. I was enjoying watching her enjoy herself. By the time we got back to her house, I could see that there was a real connection between us. But I also found out she was seeing someone. In fact, he told her that he wanted to come over.

"No, no," I heard her say to him on the phone, successfully keeping him away. She came back to me, and we talked for a long time that night. The conversation between us flowed so easily. We just clicked.

April was three years younger than me; she was still a student at the University of Southern Mississippi in Hattiesburg, Mississippi, about an hour away from Gulfport. We talked on the phone frequently, growing ever closer. I brought her out to Denver, and we became intimate. But since I was still technically married, I wanted to keep our relationship under wraps. I was new to Islam, still learning the religion and how I was supposed to live my life. I hadn't yet adopted the kind of disciplined lifestyle I would eventually come to embrace. Hey, change doesn't happen overnight.

One time during that summer I wanted to see her so badly that I hopped in my Range Rover and headed toward Hattiesburg, twenty hours away. I couldn't wait until the next day for a flight; I just drove straight there. In my mind, I was showing April I was a different kind of dude.

I didn't tell her that I was coming to visit. When I got there, her roommate told me she had gone out but would be back soon.

"When she comes back, tell her to go into her room to get something for you," I said.

She nodded excitedly. I went into April's room to wait. When she arrived, I could hear her talking to the roommate. Luckily, she didn't say anything I wasn't supposed to hear. She walked into the room and almost lost it when she saw me. She was so happy, so surprised, so excited.

I enjoyed her company so much that I would do romantic things on a whim, like fly her into Denver for a weekend or make a quick trip to Hattiesburg or Gulfport to see her. Things were going extremely well between us as we became closer and closer. But as I got deeper into my study of Islam, one day I read something that shook me. It said that divorce is detestable in the sight of Allah, but it is permissible as long as you've tried everything you can to make it work. If you've done that and you still feel like it won't work, then divorce it is. I sat back and thought about my relationship with my wife. I asked myself, *Did you really exhaust every possibility?* I had no choice but to shake my head no. I had not.

With dread, I picked up the phone and called April.

"Listen, I know we've been spending time with each other and things have gotten intense," I said. "I'm trying to be the best Muslim I can be, and I'm not perfect." I took a deep breath. "I read something that's pricking my conscience. It said that divorce is detestable in the sight of Allah, but it's permissible if you've exhausted everything. I don't feel I've done that. So, I think I got to go give it another shot. I got to make sure that I come out of it feeling that I've exhausted everything."

She didn't have a lot to say in response, but I could tell that she was hurt. That was painful to me, but I felt I had no choice since I was working toward becoming a more devoted Muslim.

"I apologize, but I have to do this," I said before we hung up.

I reconnected with Kim, and we did more talking about what was happening between us. But it soon became clear to me that nothing was going to change. This marriage was not going to work.

You might expect that once I'd concluded that I had exhausted all means to make my marriage work, I would quickly pick up the phone and call April. But that's not what I did. Hey, I was still a work in progress. I think the knowledge that I had hurt her with my indecisiveness stopped me from calling her right away. And I was uncertain whether she fit into my future.

Instead of calling April, I got entangled in several other relationships that were of varying levels of seriousness. I met a lady named Sharon whom I liked a lot. She was a few years older than me; we had a sizzling chemistry between us. She had many personal qualities I liked, such as the way she moved and the way she thought about the world. Then our connection intensified when she announced that she was going to become a Muslim. I began to think seriously about asking her to marry me — our relationship was that intense.

Around this time, I had a conversation with April, and I said some stuff to her that was not kind. I have a tendency at times to bypass diplomacy and be what some have called "brutally honest." If I feel like I might fail to get across the true meaning of what I'm trying to say because I'm being too subtle, I'd rather just give it to you straight and deal with the consequences later of how it made you feel. I told April that this woman I was now dating named Sharon did it for me more than she did. Thinking back on it now, all I can say is, Ouch. Over the years, I have learned to be a bit more tactful, but hey, we're all just unfinished business.

Shortly after making my dramatic pronouncement to April about how close I was to Sharon, I was extremely disturbed by something Sharon did. I won't go into the details here, but I felt it was something she couldn't come back from. What it told me was that marrying her would be a big mistake. I decided to bring the relationship to an end.

During a trip overseas, I "met" someone else. I put "met" in quotes because we never actually met. I was visiting with a Muslim family I knew in Iran, the second time I had been in the country, and they produced a photo of a gorgeous woman they thought I might be interested in getting to know. They knew I was hoping to someday remarry, ideally to a Muslim woman, so they wanted to play matchmaker.

"Wow, she's very nice-looking," I said. "Tell me about her."

They told me she was from Sudan and was studying dentistry in Bulgaria. They called her on the phone, and we exchanged information, though the communication was slow going because there was a significant language barrier between us. She spoke fluent Arabic, but her English wasn't very good. Of course, I didn't speak Arabic. When we started talking on the telephone, the conversations were fun but also difficult, as we tried to figure out what the other was saying. I decided I needed to take a trip to Bulgaria to see if there was anything real between us. It was a month or so before the end of the season; I planned to make the trip in the summer. In the midst of my planning, the anthem controversy exploded. Suddenly, I had much more pressing matters on my plate. But we continued to communicate, though we seemed to miss each other more than we connected.

During one of our conversations, she told me she had seen me on television. Apparently, the anthem controversy had made its way to Bulgaria. I could tell by her voice that she was excited. I thought she was a bit too excited. Even though I had told her I played basketball

as a profession, I don't think she fully grasped what that meant. It was
something I often encountered when I traveled overseas.

"What do you do?" somebody would ask me.

"I play basketball," I'd respond.

"No, no, no. What do you *do*?" they'd repeat. "For a living?"
As if I played basketball as a hobby.

I would say, "Professional basketball. In America. A lot
of money!"

"Ohh!" They usually had heard of the big money in the NBA.
After all, Michael Jordan was by then a global phenomenon.

Until she saw me on TV, I think my friend in Bulgaria hadn't
understood the nature of my profession — or the fame and money
associated with it. Google didn't exist. It would have taken considerable effort for her to do the research to find out these details
about my life. But after she found out about my fame, I had become
another person in her mind. I could hear it in her voice. It was a turn-
off and reminded me of previous women who started acting differently, caught up in the materialism, when they realized who I was. I
began to have my doubts about making the trip to Bulgaria.

After Coach Bickerstaff told me to forget about the rest of the 1996
season — my sixth in the NBA — I got a surprise call one day as I sat
in my home in Denver. It was from April. She said she had heard
there were death threats against me and she just wanted to make
sure I was okay. Her voice had a calming influence on me. We began
talking again; it felt like we clicked even more than we had before.
She was even sounding more receptive to embracing Islam. That
turned me on. I was starting to feel confused. I had gotten close to
three different women in a short amount of time, though one of them
I hadn't yet met in person. My heart was pulled in several directions
at once. *What should I do?*

With my emotions in upheaval, I went upstairs to the *musalla*, the huge prayer room I had built in my house. There was a *wudu* station, where Muslims cleanse the body before prayer. Mine had three separate stalls for washing up. I had a full library connected to the prayer room, which was overflowing with books. When you stepped into the room, the floor was covered with prayer rugs. I went into the room and prepared to make a prayer called *istikhara*.

Salat al-Istikhaara, which translates to Prayer of Seeking Counsel, is a prayer recited by Muslims who need guidance from God when facing a difficult decision in their life. Muslims are cautioned that they shouldn't make istikhara unless they are willing to follow whatever guidance comes to them as a result of the prayer. Even if the guidance is pushing you toward the decision you didn't want to make, you aren't to resist.

During my prayer, I told Allah I wanted to get married, but I wasn't sure which way to go. "Please make it clear to me who I should be with — or none of them."

Almost instantly after I made istikhara, I couldn't get April off my mind. No matter where I went, no matter what I was doing, there was April, perched in my head. I tried to fight it by telling myself that although I thought she was lovely, she didn't look like the Hollywood models that popular culture and the media were signaling a professional athlete like me should be choosing. *She's pretty, but she ain't like that image I have in my mind.* I'd feel bad about thinking that, though, and I'd follow it up with all the qualities she had that I loved, like her loyalty and affection and the way we moved so easily together. It kept hitting me, and I kept trying to push her away. *No, she can't be the one! She can't be!* But every time I pushed, it would just come back and hit me harder. I got to the point where I could not envision my life without her. Finally, I surrendered. I had made istikhara and Allah had given me my answer. That was that.

I didn't go to Bulgaria. Instead, I traveled down to Mississippi after the season ended. I went to see April at her parents' home. I told her that I liked how we were together, but I needed to know for sure whether we worked as a couple for a sustained period. Could she come to Denver and spend a few weeks with me at my home? She said she didn't mind at all, though she added I had to get her father's approval. I went in search of her father. I talked to the whole family separately — her father, her mother, her sister, and her brother.

"I'm interested in your daughter," I said, looking at her father and then the rest of the family. "I don't know where this is going to end up, but I would like to give it a heightened chance of succeeding." I leaned in. This was the big one. "I would like for April to come back to Denver with me. It will give us a chance to be more confident about our relationship, by being able to see each other in that environment. We can be around each other to see if we have that chemistry. If she's living with me, she can see how I operate, I can see how she operates."

When I paused and looked around at them, I didn't see any scowls. So far, so good.

"I know she'll be giving up her job to go to Denver. We've already talked, and I'm willing to make sure that she's comfortable, so that before she even gets to me she doesn't feel like, 'Oh, I'm leaving my job, and what if it doesn't work out? Do I have to start all over again?' We've already talked about it, and I told her that I'll give her enough money where she won't have to worry about that. She can feel comfortable about it, that if she left, she's good."

I was seeing nods of agreement now.

"She wanted me to come talk to you," I said. "I also think it's necessary, 'cause we want to know if we have your blessings."

Her father looked at me closely, then he nodded. "You have my blessing," he said.

Her mother said the same thing, as did her sister and her brother. Within days, we were together in Denver, in my home.

A few days later, I had to travel to Washington, D.C., to speak at a fundraiser for a Muslim organization there. April and I stayed with a person who is like a father I never had, Salahuddeen Abdul Kareem and his wife, Sister Hanifa, at their home.

After the event, before we got in the car to return to their home, Sister Hanifa said to me, quite mysteriously, "You know, Sister April's got something to tell you."

I jokingly said during the car ride, "I'm not nervous. I didn't do anything."

When we got back to their place, April and I went down to the basement for some privacy. I saw that April had tears in her eyes. She began softly sobbing. What in the world was going on?

"I want to be a Muslim," she said between tears.

Whoa. I didn't expect that. April was not the kind of person to do things she didn't want to do just to please somebody else, even me. If she was saying something like this, I knew she meant it. I didn't second-guess her at all. If she was just doing it to win me over, she could have made such a declaration much earlier when we were starting to get to know each other. She had been brought up Catholic and had become disenchanted with her faith. She had been looking; she now believed she had found what she was looking for. It made sense.

"You sure?" I asked. She was crying, so I needed to fully understand what was happening. "You sure this is what you want to do? You don't want to think it over? I mean, I'm not forcing you or compelling you to do anything."

"No, my decision is made," she responded. "I'm crying because I'm happy."

Though she was joyful about her decision, I think she also was crying because she was concerned about what her family was going to think, though her family must have thought this was a strong possibility when we became a couple.

When we were together, I enjoyed her vibe, her personality, everything about her. I couldn't imagine being without her. So, when she said she wanted to become Muslim, I knew in that moment that I was going to ask her to marry me. After we returned to Denver, I told her I had to run a quick errand and left the house. I went to the jewelry store to shop for a ring. There was one that spoke to me above the others. It wasn't anything extravagant; no enormous monstrosity that would attract all kinds of unwanted attention. I paid less than fifteen grand for it, but the diamond was extremely clear, pristine. I left the jewelry store and went to another store to buy her a headscarf that she could wear after her reversion to Islam. I asked the salesclerk if she could weave the scarf around the ring so that the ring would be sitting on top of it when April opened the box.

When I got back home, I brought her out on the balcony of the bedroom where we slept.

"I bought you something," I said. I could see the anticipation on her face.

I presented her with the box. Because it contained the scarf, it was bigger than a ring box, thus concealing my intentions.

"Oh?" she said.

When she opened it and saw the ring sitting on top, her eyes widened. She looked at me and then she looked down at it again.

"Aaaaahhh!" she started screaming.

"Will you marry me?" I asked, as smooth as can be.

"Aaaaaahhh!"

"I said, will you marry me?" I repeated.

"Aaaaaahhh!"

"Hey, you need to answer me," I said, smiling.

"Yesss!" she said.

We embraced and kissed. Then she had to get to the important stuff: she went to call her mother. There was all kinds of excitement in the air.

I had been traded to the Sacramento Kings, and I wanted to have the wedding before I left for training camp. We had only a few weeks to get it done. I made arrangements to have the ceremony in Castle Rock, a cozy town outside of Denver that is named for the castle-shaped rock formation at the top of a small mountain in the center of town. I didn't want to have it in Mississippi, so I paid for both of our families to make the trip to Denver. It was a lovely, modest ceremony. I didn't believe in paying huge sums for a wedding — money that could be put to much better use during our marriage.

Just a few days after the wedding, April and I made the trip to Sacramento, and we found a place to stay in this new city for us, in the middle of California. All the while, I was thinking about acclimating myself with a new team after the ridiculous spectacle of the previous season. I only hoped that I wouldn't step into this new situation with unnecessary drama.

I was enjoying my time with April so much that my heart wasn't into basketball. It just wasn't high on my list of priorities anymore. I was much more into reading things that piqued my interest, spending time with my wife, and thinking about starting a family. April and I were extremely close. She told me often that I always made her feel special. I let her know just as often how much I loved and appreciated her and how much I treasured her commitment and loyalty.

But I also felt I had been blessed by Allah with this gift, my ability to put a ball through a net; I didn't want to reject God's favors. But it was getting harder for me to concentrate. I just wanted to be a better Muslim. Part of that was being more socially active and doing work to help make the world a better place, to fight against injustice. Basketball didn't easily fit into that picture for me.

With all these thoughts racing through my mind, the most obvious manifestation of my waning interest is that I gained weight again. I went into training camp out of shape, which was the worst thing I could have done to establish myself on this new team. It had been more than a decade since the Sacramento Kings finished with a winning record, though the team had made the playoffs the previous season with a record of 39–43, only to lose in the first round to Seattle.

On top of everything else, we had been in Sacramento only a short while when April told me that she was pregnant. I was ecstatic. I was about to realize my lifelong dream of having my own family. That made it even harder to concentrate on basketball, to leave my pregnant wife at home while I traveled around the country. But a few months into the pregnancy, we got devastating news: April had had a miscarriage. This was difficult news to accept, as I imagined it would be for any expecting parent. So much was happening in my life that my focus on basketball just wasn't there. Basketball, which used to be my refuge, my safe place, had become an unwelcome chore.

I was hopeful that I would get a fair shot in Sacramento, but it didn't take long after I got there to be reminded of the anthem controversy. We were having a team meeting after training camp had started. One of the team officials said he wanted to go through the rule book with us. The NBA had made an addition since the previous season. Before, there was no actual rule about the national anthem, as Rod Thorn told my agent in the midst of the controversy. But now, in big bold letters, there was a section called "National Anthem" in which the league stipulated that players must now stand. I had already come up with a compromise in Denver: standing, but holding my hands in prayer. I would continue doing that in Sacramento.

When the team official read that section, everyone turned to look at me. I stared back at them and smirked. Then I laughed, which caused everybody else to laugh, defusing any tension. I hoped that was the end of my association with the national anthem. Unfortunately, that hope was naive. Eventually I learned that I likely would be associated with the national anthem for the rest of my life.

That first season with the Kings was up and down. I had some outstanding 20-plus-point games in which the baskets came in bunches. There were sixteen games in which I scored 20 or more, two in which I scored more than 30. But I also had too many games where I didn't play much. Even though I was too heavy, I could still get my shot off when I wanted, even if it was sometimes harder to get to my spot. In that first season in Sacramento, I started fifty-one games and finished with a per game scoring average of 13.7 — the second-highest average on the team behind Mitch Richmond, who averaged 25.9, fourth highest in the league. The team finished a disappointing 34–48, sixth place in the Pacific division, just above the last-place Golden State Warriors. I don't mind pointing out that the Denver Nuggets finished that season with a record of 21–61.

Little did I realize that the fifty-one games I started that first season would look like a big year compared with the next season. Under Coach Eddie Jordan, a former NBA player, I didn't start a single game and appeared in only thirty-one games. I had two consecutive games early in the season when I scored 20 points even though I played less than thirty minutes in both games. It was by far the low point of my basketball life up to then. Game after game, I wouldn't even get up off the bench. Talk about a fall from grace. It was painful and infuriating.

When we traveled to Denver for a game in early February, I found out the root of my problem in Sacramento. The news actually came by way of my brother Omar. He was still living in Denver with his young family. I invited him to the game, so he sat in the family section. But because they had never seen him before, the Sacramento staff had no idea who he was. At the end of the game, which the

Kings won, 101–99, Omar heard Head Coach Garry St. Jean talking to some NBA people who were at the game. He was eavesdropping, and he heard an earful.

"Hey, brother, I need to tell you something," he said when he caught up with me.

"What? What's happening?"

"I was over there by one of the coaches and he was talking to some people. He was talking about your minutes and why you weren't being played," Omar said. "He said, 'There's a reason behind that.' He told them that he has to find a way to not play you so much. He said as long as Mahmoud is in with Mitch, Mitch doesn't get enough attempts."

I shook my head. It made a lot of sense. It's not that I wasn't producing; they couldn't risk making Mitch Richmond unhappy. Mitch was a perennial NBA All-Star and future Hall of Famer (he got inducted in 2014). He was the face of the franchise. They had to sacrifice me and my minutes to make sure he got enough shots to stay content. I'm not saying Mitch was aware of all this. I doubt he was. But it was a window into the unsightly underbelly of the business of basketball that the fans rarely see.

Not long after that, somebody came to me and told me what Rudy Tomjanovich, the legendary Houston Rockets coach (who was inducted into the Hall of Fame in 2020), said in the locker room after we played the Rockets.

"Why aren't they playing Mahmoud?" I was told he said to a group of journalists. "When we come here, we organize our defenses around stopping him."

As the season came to a close, I could see the proverbial writing on the wall. My time in Sacramento was a wrap — pointless, painful, and unlikely to improve. My two-year deal, which totaled about $3.3 million, was ending. If I re-signed, I knew the Kings would try to get me on the cheap, using my second season there as proof of my worth—as proof that I no longer had it. I had made it easier for them by not being in tip-top shape, but I certainly didn't deserve to spend an entire NBA season on the bench. I was only twenty-nine years old—still at the height of my basketball prime. I needed to go somewhere I would be appreciated.

When I observed what they did to 49ers quarterback Colin Kaepernick during the controversy over him kneeling for the anthem, it felt very familiar. Play with his minutes, put him in, take him out, mess up his rhythm, hurt his performance—all to justify their claim that he doesn't have it anymore, that he's not the same player. Colin and I were not the first professional athletes to suffer through that; unfortunately, we probably won't be the last. In the business of professional sports, we are commodities to be invested in—and then dumped when they think we have become liabilities by speaking our minds and standing up for ourselves.

I made a decision to flee the treachery of the NBA and try my luck overseas. With the help of my agent, Sharif Naseer, I signed a contract with a team in Istanbul, Turkey, called Fenerbahçe, which was part of the EuroLeague, the top basketball league in Europe. I signed a contract for more than $1 million a year, including a $600,000 bonus that they gave me before I left for Europe.

I played in Turkey for just three months, from the end of 1998 into the beginning of 1999. Though I wasn't that pleased with what was happening on the court and within the organization, I can say in retrospect that most of my problems were personal and didn't have much to do with Turkey or the team. I was losing my love for the game, partly because of my growing interest in my faith, history, sociology, psychology, politics, you name it, and partly because I was out of shape. When you're out of shape, you just carry yourself a little differently. Your motivation is not the same. I was also annoyed by the unhealthy favoritism I saw over there, something I had always railed against—the notion of playing someone for reasons other than he was the best player for the position, which I came to learn happened a lot overseas. When American players go to play in these foreign lands, the powers that be consider it in their best interest to promote and protect their local guys, even if it means a better American player is going to not play as much. Of course, this isn't to insinuate that every person from America is better than their players because that was not the case.

The main problem was I didn't want to be there. We had found out that April was pregnant again; the last thing I wanted to do was leave my pregnant wife by herself and travel to the other side of the world to shoot a basketball.

I flew back to Gulfport in time for the birth of my first son, Ali. With him I started the tradition of cutting the umbilical cord, which I subsequently did for all my children. When a baby is born, you recite the adhan, the Muslim call to prayer, in the baby's right ear and the iqama, the second call to prayer, in the other ear. This was what I had dreamed of when I first started playing basketball. It was the thought that drove me during those 5:00 A.M. training sessions near the shores of the Gulf in Mississippi. My own family. I was twenty-nine years old, and it finally had arrived.

I felt so overwhelmed with joy and blessings when I held my son in my arms. I had a hard time putting into words all the emotions that were flowing through me. Not only did I feel ecstatic, grateful, and humbled at this phenomenal thing that had just happened, but I was also scared, apprehensive. Not scared in the sense of the bogeyman type of scared, but scared about the future. I knew what kind of world he was coming into. Being Black, being Muslim, I couldn't help but think about the challenges he would face. I was holding this lovely human being, and I wanted to give him all the love that I could, educate him as much as possible. I was download-ing all my hopes into him. While life has its challenges, it is also beautiful. I wanted him to experience all that beauty, to see how amazing life could be.

To my undying chagrin, a couple days after Ali's birth I had to get back on a plane and return to Turkey, leaving behind my wife and newborn son. It was an extremely painful trip. During the flight, I grappled with difficult thoughts. *Man, I got to fly back over this ocean — what if this is my last day on Earth?*

It was similar to those thoughts I would have when I was younger, but now there was a substantial urgency to it because I had a family to think about. I was actually tearful as I sat in my seat. I wanted to be the best father I could be, especially after not having one of my own, but the first thing I had done was leave my son and travel far away from him. *What kind of father does that?*

When I got to Turkey, all I could think about was leaving. Playing basketball was the furthest thing from my mind. However, I still regret the immature way I handled my departure. When I decided to leave after just three months, they told me I had to return the $600,000 bonus they had given me. They had taken my passport when I arrived in Istanbul, so I couldn't leave without their consent. They wanted the $600,000 back. In my mind, the $600,000 was the cost of doing business — you win some, you lose some. In this case, because I didn't want to play anymore, they lost. But that's not how the team saw it.

"You owe us money," one of the team execs said to me.

"I don't owe you anything," I said.

"You signed a contract, right?"

But I wouldn't budge. The $600,000 was an advance bonus, not my payment for playing. At least that's the way I was thinking at the time. If I was more mature, I would have paid them back a portion of the $600,000. That would have been the ethical thing. But in my anger, I wasn't thinking ethically. When they threatened to keep my passport, I called their bluff.

"No problem—I love this country!" I said. "I'll be here as long as you like." I did enjoy the country, which made it easier to say that.

They looked at me like I was crazy. It was all so foolish, how I acted. Though the owner was Muslim, I had no idea what kind of man I was dealing with. I was in their country, and there was a whole lot of money on the table. People have gotten killed for far less. I heard a story about another NBA player, a guard who had signed with a team in Russia. Something went down and he ended up owing them a bunch of money. Enforcer-type guys came and knocked on his door. Mind you, this was after he had left their country and was playing now in the NBA. He was fortunate he had the money, so he paid them the hundreds of thousands he owed and continued his career.

I confronted a similar scenario in Istanbul when I got visited by a couple of possible hit men. I lived in a high-rise apartment building. They said they wanted to meet with me. I didn't want to be alone with them in my apartment, so I told them I would come downstairs. I wanted to be in a public place with people around. So, we talked in the parking lot. I was standing up, with two very large guys standing nearby, while the owner sat in his car. I told him I was unhappy and didn't want to play anymore.

"You can just tear up the contract," I said.

"Well, we gave you a lot of money," the owner said. "It's only right that if you're not going to play, you return the money."

What he was saying was right, but I wasn't trying to hear him. By that point I was just mad that they were trying to keep me there, like I was a prisoner or something. I wasn't thinking rationally.

In my mind, an advance is a guaranteed payment whether you go on to play or not. But in retrospect that thinking was wrong.

I stayed in Turkey for about three more weeks. They finally returned my passport and let me go home. As an illustration of how immature I was at the time, right before I left, I deliberately drove the rental car they had given me to the far side of Istanbul and parked it in one of the country's busiest regions, where millions of people lived. I wanted to make it hard for them to find the car. Then I flew out the next day. The whole saga is one of those things you look back on later in life and seriously regret how you acted. The fact that I made it back home to my family in one piece was a blessing.

had a joyful time in 2000 watching my son grow from a newborn into a lovely little person. I was grateful for the precious uninterrupted months with my family. But I had to admit I was worried about the state of my career. At thirty years old, I knew I was still in my prime. When I was in shape, humbly speaking, I felt there weren't many people on the planet who could stop me. However, I didn't know if I would ever get another chance to prove that. I knew my religious beliefs and my principles had marked me as "difficult." I hoped there were people in the league who would understand that those things had little to do with my basketball skills. But perhaps that was naive. I would come to discover that I couldn't avoid the forces off the basketball court working against me and my career.

I was pleased when I got a phone call from Orlando before the 2000 season started, asking if I had any interest in playing for the Magic. But when I began talks with the Magic, I didn't like what I was hearing. I told them that I would be interested, but only if they could assure me that if I reported to camp in tip-top shape and proceeded to perform at a high level, then I would play. I felt that I still had a lot to offer. But they resisted giving me that guarantee, which I found strange and off-putting. You mean, if I'm in shape and I'm killing it on the floor, you still can't say that I would play? I got an unsettled feeling, like I'd be going to Orlando to occupy a place on the bench, like Sacramento all over again, and becoming a what-happened-to-him scenario and justifying in some people's minds the idea that I couldn't play anymore.

It reminded me of when I was being recruited out of high school by Georgetown. Craig Esherick, a Georgetown assistant coach, arrived before the legendary coach John Thompson, who had caught a later flight to Mississippi. Esherick sat in my living room and told me that when I got to Georgetown, I wouldn't play right away. Instead I should go to class, maintain my grades, and wait for my chance. "All right?" he said.

I was respectful, so I didn't object, but inside I was broiling. I was the number one guard coming out of high school in the entire country, and he was telling me I had to sit on the bench, even if I was better than everybody else on the team? Nah, that wasn't going to work for me. I thought that was wrong. Esherick killed the deal before Coach Thompson even got to Mississippi.

Now I was hearing something similar from Orlando. They were offering me over a million dollars, so I would be well compensated. I certainly could have used the money. I had gone an entire year without any income. A million dollars sounded real nice to my ears. But I just couldn't pull the trigger; I couldn't go to Florida and sit on the bench. That couldn't be my NBA legacy, being stashed in mothballs at age thirty. I told them thank you, but no thank you. I said that's not what I was looking for.

I got a phone call a bit later from a friend, Hashim Alauddeen, who was one of my first Islamic teachers. At the time he was attending school at the University of California at Berkeley; he's now an imam.

"Hey, man, if I could get you to Vancouver, would you go?" he asked.

I wasn't in on the details of what he did, but he pulled a Don King move of sorts. He called Dick Versace, the Vancouver Grizzlies' president of basketball operations, and told him about how I had dominated at an exhibition game in Mississippi against a bunch of top pros who were in town. The Grizzlies were looking for playmakers, so they gave me a call.

What Versace didn't know was that my friend Hashim had embellished the story quite a bit. I did play well in the game, but the competition wasn't exactly top pros. There were very good players in the game, some of whom were about to go play college basketball. I was matched up against Joezon Darby, who had recently played for Ole Miss. Darby, who is still a friend of mine, and I were trading baskets back and forth. I might have finished with 30 points or so, but I was terribly out of shape. Even though the shots were going in, I felt sluggish. Slow.

Based partly on Hashim's recommendation, the Grizzlies flew me up to Vancouver. I got a surprise when I got on the elevator and saw that Versace was already on it. Right away, he brought up the game in Mississippi, mentioning that he had heard there were "top pros" playing. I didn't want to lie about the level of competition, but I also didn't want to mess up my boy. I was kind of stuck. I came up with a creative way of having it both ways.

"Oh yeah, there were some top-notch players there," I said. "We had some fun."

I never said the word *pros*. Versace looked at me closely, perhaps noticing the hesitation in my voice. Thankfully, he let it drop.

During the meeting, they questioned me about how I would deal with the flag if it came up. I had already resigned myself to the likelihood that the anthem issue would follow me whenever I played in the United States.

"The same way I dealt with it before I left," I said.

I guess that answer was acceptable, because they offered me a two-year deal. However, I decided not to take the two years. I told them to give me one year and let me show them that I still could dominate on the court. Instead of being locked into a second year below my value, I decided I was going to take a chance on myself. I would get in shape and, barring injuries, impress on the floor.

Even though they gave me just under a million for that one year, in retrospect I should have taken the two-year deal because they did not live up to their word. There's a part of me that is always betting on the fairness and kindness of humans, even though I've had experiences in the past where people have lied to me and cheated me. Versace and his staff assured me that I would play if I deserved to play, so I believed them.

I worked hard before reporting to camp, dropping weight and feeling light on my feet once again. In team scrimmages, I was dominating, getting my shots whenever I wanted. *Yes, this is going to be a good year.*

Man, was I wrong. I didn't get on the floor until the fourth game of the season; I played less than six minutes and got off one shot, which I missed. In the first twenty games of the season, I played in just five of them, scoring a total of 6 points. It felt ridiculous to me. Throughout the entire season, I never started a game. The most minutes I logged in a game was twenty-three minutes, against Houston in the third-to-last game of the season. I scored 25 points in those twenty-three minutes, which was my season high. The team was investing most of the point guard minutes in Mike Bibby, who had won an NCAA championship with Arizona and whom the Grizzlies had picked second in the NBA draft a couple years earlier.

Toward the end of the season, while I was sitting on the bench during a game, I had an interesting conversation with one of my teammates, Michael Dickerson. Dickerson was a shooting guard out of Arizona who was the second leading scorer on the team behind the big fella, Shareef Abdur-Rahim. Dickerson was in his third year in the league at the time; his career was cut short because of injuries a few years later.

"Mahmoud, did you know that of all the people in the NBA right now, including Jordan, you're averaging more points per minute than anybody in the league?" he said to me. "When you get in, you average a point a minute."

Because I hardly played, I wasn't keeping track of my statistics. But when Dickerson told me that, I got pissed. Not long after that conversation with Dickerson, I got called into a meeting with Dick Versace. We exchanged a bit of small talk before we got into it. Versace had a request: he asked if I would go on injured reserve temporarily to make room for another player. I had already been told that this might happen.

"No," I said. "Ask somebody else."

Versace eyed me but didn't say anything.

"Listen. Before I came here, we had a conversation," I said. "The conversation was that if I came here and I got into the shape I was supposed to be in, then you were going to play me. I know that Bibby is your guy. He's young and you're grooming him. I understand the business, whether I agree or not. But I don't understand sitting behind some of these other guys. We had an agreement and you haven't honored that agreement." I paused. "I've done everything under the sun to get to the shape I'm supposed to be in. Your coaches, your staff, the players are saying, 'Mahmoud is dominating practice.' This should be the barometer for who gets into the game. But I can't seem to get into the game." I shook my head. "And now you want me to go on the injured list to make room for another player? Nah.

"You're not a man of your word," I added.

He nodded. "You know what? You're right. I'm not," he said. "But when we brought you in, you didn't even have to try out after sitting out those seasons."

"That's not my problem," I said. "That wasn't our conversation. That didn't have anything to do with what we talked about. I understand and appreciate that, but we had an agreement and you're not honoring it."

We went back and forth for a long while, talking about the team and my place on it. I began to soften a bit.

"Listen. Let's say that I end up accepting this arrangement and I go on the injured list. How am I to trust that you're going to keep your word since you haven't thus far — that I'm not going to stay on there the whole year?"

We still had more than a month to go in the season. The team was seriously struggling at the time; we had just lost fourteen of the last sixteen games, including our last five in a row.

"Look, you have my word," he said.

"Okay, I'm going to try it one more time, to see if you're going to keep your word."

Versace nodded. The meeting had lasted a lot longer than I expected — about forty minutes. I walked out of his office unsure of what this all meant for my future with the Grizzlies.

He did keep his word. I stayed on the injured list for about three weeks, a total of nine games. During that stretch, we lost seven games and won two. Keeping me out of uniform clearly was not the key to success, though just having me in uniform didn't help us win, either. Based on my performance during practice and when I got substantial playing time in games, I believe I demonstrated I could have made a difference.

Around that time I had an impromptu meeting with Sidney Lowe, the head coach. Sidney had played in the league a few years after winning a national championship as the point guard for North Carolina State. He had been an assistant coach on several NBA teams before being named head coach in Vancouver.

We had a conversation in the gym one day after practice. Sidney wasn't a bad guy; he was in a difficult position.

"Mahmoud, we're not doing you right," Sidney said, not for the first time. "I'm going to find time to put you in."

"Listen, Sidney," I said. "It's obvious you don't have any power. You don't have any control. Just give it to me straight up. Don't tell me you're going to do something if you're not going to do it. I would respect you more as a man if you just tell me, 'Mahmoud, it's beyond my control. I would love to play you, but my hands are tied.' I wouldn't agree with that, but I'd understand. And I'd respect you more for being straight up."

He didn't have much to say in response. But I could see what was going on. Though the Grizzlies had brought me in, they had little to no interest in ensuring my success with the club. In the last game of the season, on April 18, 2001, in Oakland against the Golden State Warriors, I played a total of twenty-one minutes and scored 14 points. They would be the last points I ever scored in the NBA. External forces blew in like a storm, changing the path of my life and career.

A few months after the season ended, I got a call at about 4:00 A.M. from a Muslim sister in our community named Ivy. "Are you looking at the television?" she asked. "Because your house is burning down."

I turned on the news and immediately saw footage of a fire at the house we were building in Kiln, Mississippi, about forty minutes from Gulfport. I found it interesting that I hadn't gotten a call from the police or anybody official. I had to hear about the fire from somebody in the community. I got dressed and drove out to the scene, which was still swarming with firefighters.

The 8,200-square-foot house, with six bedrooms, six bathrooms, and a theater room, was supposed to be our dream home. But it had been the scene of troubling events almost since we first broke ground. When the house was still in the framing process, somebody in a large vehicle (it had left deep and wide tire prints) rammed into the garage doors. After the outside walls had been built and finished, somebody painted the KKK insignia in three different places around the house.

Kiln, which is where Brett Favre is from, was known to the Black community as a racist place. But in my mind, the whole world is racist, so that wasn't a reason to reject the location. Besides, the land was perfect for what I wanted to do. It was fifty-three acres and right off the main road. My plan was to create a gated, self-sufficient community; we could have cattle, farms, and fish in the lovely pond. Our house would be surrounded by others in the community, people I had persuaded to build homes there. I thought it was a great idea. But the only problem was it would have taken a while to build it out, and in the meantime my family would have been there solo for quite a while. Even after the fire I still wanted to build the house. But with me traveling so much, I didn't want to take the risk of leaving my family there and having something happen to them.

After the fire, I got a visit from the FBI in the masjid that we had built in the Black neighborhood in Gulfport. They were trying to determine if it was a hate crime. But the authorities decided there wasn't enough evidence to give them an answer. I settled with the insurance company. Case closed.

Building the masjid in Gulfport was an act of love, grace, and mercy. At the time I was living with my family in Pass Christian, which was about twenty minutes away. It was an abandoned motel that housed people with drug addictions; I purchased it and turned it into a prayer house. Before that, we had been having services at a small house I bought on Twenty-Second Street, not far from where I grew up. We would hold classes there, in addition to Friday jum'ah services. As our Muslim community grew, I knew we needed more space; African Americans from the community were reverting to

Islam, and Muslim immigrants were moving into Gulfport. When I
saw the former motel, I knew it would be a great spot for us. It's a
two-story, 3,200-square-foot building. We put a little gym on the second floor, where we also have classrooms. The first floor is the masjid
area where we pray. It has become a warm, welcoming place that has
brought me great pride.

Not long after the fire, the nation was devastated by the
deadly attacks on the World Trade Center and the Pentagon. Since
the media was reporting that the perpetrators were Muslim, HBO
wanted to get my take. I got an invitation to appear on *Real Sports
with Bryant Gumbel.* Not one to shy away from the tough questions,
I decided to accept the invitation. But the interview with *Real Sports*
correspondent Bernard Goldberg turned out to be the final fatal blow
to my NBA career.

Before the interview, Goldberg and his crew drove around
Gulfport with me as we talked and got to know each other. I took
them to the masjid and out to the property that had been burned
down. I got a sense that Goldberg—a well-known conservative who
later went on to work for Fox News—was coming at me with an
agenda, almost like he was going to try to sabotage me. I knew he
was going to get into the 9/11 attack, so I went back home and dug
into my notes and did some reading, publications like the *Socialist
Review, Crescent International,* and *Washington Report on Middle East
Affairs*—not exactly mainstream, but well respected in progressive
and Muslim circles. I decided I wasn't going to be diplomatic; if
he asked me something, I was going to tell him what I thought, no
holds barred.

We sat down in the masjid in the musalla, the area where we
conduct congregational prayers. Usually when journalists interview
you, they start by asking you very general questions: How's your
family? How's everything going? But Goldberg didn't do that. He

looked at me with a sly but serious look on his face and asked, "So, do you think bin Laden did it?" That was his first question.

I chuckled and told him that my information led me to believe he hadn't masterminded the 9/11 attacks, but if he had, he didn't do it alone. From there, the interview quickly became contentious, with Goldberg constantly challenging me on the sources of my information. I gave him a laundry list of questionable items surrounding the 9/11 attacks, such as Israeli prime minister Ariel Sharon being asked by his security advisers not to show up that day, people who some said were Mossad agents filming the entire incident from a rooftop in New Jersey, billions of dollars in stock market trades the day before the attack involving those particular airlines.

"Don't you think this is valuable information? Don't you think the public should be privy to this?" I said to him.

We went at it, back and forth. He would sometimes switch subjects to my house burning down or my anthem controversy. At one point he asked me, "Well, what is it that you don't like about America?"

"In almost every war, if not every war, that's generated in the world, America has its hands in it," I said. "It has bases all over the world. But no other country can have a base here, right?"

He said that these were foreign examples. What were some domestic examples?

"This is considered a melting pot, am I right?" I said. "When people that live in these countries become aware of the fact that when their mamas and their daddies and nieces and nephews and cousins are being bombed and killed and raped, their resources and lands are being destroyed and stolen, as a result of what America is doing, it produces the effects of what we have on 9/11."

Two different times he cut the interview short and went outside with his producer. I could see out the window that he was cursing the guy out. I think he was upset because in the preinterviews I did over the phone with *Real Sports*, I didn't tell them any of this stuff. I had done enough interviews to know that when they call you beforehand to ask you questions, you don't give them everything. I had saved some for myself and he wasn't ready for it—and he wasn't happy about that.

At one point he asked me where I was getting my information from. I gave him a list, though I left out the Muslim publications because I figured he would have said they are biased sources. Instead, I told him the *Washington Report on Middle East Affairs* and *Socialist Review*. He had no response. I also said that the corporate media industry he works for surely gets all this information.

"You just choose to ignore it and present what you want or [what] you deem satisfactory to your sponsors," I said.

"You know, a lot of people think you're crazy," he said.

"Look, man, I'm not intimidated by that," I said. "All the prophets, scripturally, were viewed as crazy. Even though I'm striving to follow in their footsteps, I'm certainly not likening myself to them. I'm not intimidated nor deterred by that statement. I'm honored by it. Imam Musa once told me that if you pick up the paper and your enemies are saying good things about you, you're doing something wrong. If they're condemning you and calling you names, you must be doing something right."

I looked him in his eyes. "Listen. I don't care what you or anybody else thinks. I've made a decision that I'm going to live and die with a free conscience and a free soul, whether you or anybody likes it or not. So let the chips fall wherever they may."

He said something else that was telling: "You know, what you are saying will most likely mess up your chances of returning to the NBA to play again."

I responded, "I'm well aware of that, but if you think I'm going to compromise my integrity and belief system for a paycheck, then you are crazy."

When we were done, as he reached his hand out to me to shake, he said, "Regardless of what people may say, you are a man among men."

I returned with the same sly grin he gave me earlier.

As Goldberg and his crew were leaving, I could sense that the interview was going to be butchered to make me look as bad as possible. When it aired, I saw that my sense had been correct. It was edited to make me look radical and dangerous.

After that interview ran, I couldn't even get an NBA team to talk to me. My agent called around the league and there was absolutely no interest. He talked to the president of the Phoenix Suns, Jerry Colangelo. Even before he could go into his pitch about me, Colangelo cut him off.

"We're not interested, and it has nothing to do with basketball, either," he said.

People around me had tried to get me to play in the NBA Summer League, but I was adamantly opposed to it. I said, "Man, look, they already know what I can do. Why should I have to go to something like that to prove myself?"

The next summer, in 2002, I did decide to go down to Houston to participate in the informal scrimmages that a lot of the NBA guys played in to stay sharp. Because some of the guys might not be attached to a team, NBA scouts and even coaches would show up at these scrimmages. My game hadn't fallen off at all; I played pretty well, showing that I could still get my shots against NBA-caliber competition. I had scouts from the Los Angeles Lakers and the San Antonio Spurs tell me that I looked like I hadn't lost a step. I didn't say much in response; I just listened. San Antonio ended up inviting me to a summer training camp they were running.

When I got to San Antonio and walked into the facility, I noticed right away that I was getting cold looks from one of the coaches, P. J. Carlesimo, who had just been hired as an assistant by Head Coach Gregg Popovich. Carlesimo had been all over the news a few years earlier when he was the head coach for the Golden State Warriors and got choked by Latrell Sprewell at practice. You can tell when you walk in a room and somebody has a negative perception of you. Carlesimo didn't know me at all, but clearly he had been influenced by the portrait that had been painted of me in the media. Right away he seemed real standoffish, like he wasn't pleased that I was there. But over the next couple of days, something happened when he got to know me—he started to warm up. We had frequent conversations, and he started smiling around me. He never came right out and said it, but I could tell that he must have changed his mind about me.

I didn't get offered a spot with San Antonio, but I did get invited to another short camp where I'd be competing with NBA-level guys. I played well again and got approached by an assistant with the Los Angeles Clippers.

"Hey, man, we're looking for a guard," he said. "We think you can be a fit for us. Elgin Baylor wants to talk to you."

"Sure, no problem," I said. "I'd love to talk."

We were off the next day. I went to the arena to meet with Elgin. After a Hall of Fame NBA career, Elgin had been vice president of basketball operations for the Clippers since 1986. I sat in the stands and waited. After a while, I saw that he was sitting on the opposite side of the arena, looking at me. But he didn't move. And nobody else came over to talk to me. *Okay, this is weird,* I thought. *What's taking so long?*

After several more minutes, the assistant who had spoken to me the day before walked over.

"Mahmoud, man, I just want to apologize," he said.

"For what?"

"I know we called you for this meeting. Elgin said he wanted to talk to you, but now he doesn't want to talk to you on account of what you said on HBO."

I chuckled out loud. "Look, man, no problem. I understand."

And that was it. I walked out of the arena more than a little upset. After all, they had called me there to talk to Elgin, an NBA exec who surely knew everything about me. Why would they now be telling me they didn't want to talk to me because of something I said a year earlier? But I also knew that just because Elgin was in a decision-making position didn't necessarily mean he had control over everything in the organization. Ultimately, Elgin answered to the owner of the team, who happened to be Donald Sterling. The whole country learned who Sterling was in 2014, when the NBA stripped him of ownership of the team and banned him for life after racist comments he had made about Magic Johnson were made public. I'll never know if the orders came from Sterling, but clearly somebody got to Elgin and told him he couldn't talk to me. I was just disappointed that after calling me there for a meeting, this Black man didn't have the guts to tell me himself what had happened.

The next year, after having two years to concentrate on my family and on the running of the masjid, I eventually decided to sign with a team in Russia. I spent the 2003–2004 season playing for Ural Great in Perm, Russia's fourteenth-largest city, with more than a million residents, about nine hundred miles east of Moscow. People in basketball circles now knew of my situation, that I had been shut out of the NBA. I also had a bad reputation overseas because of what happened in Turkey. As a result, I was forced to play for crumbs. I had to prove in Russia that my problems in Turkey had been personal, not because I had a problem playing outside the United States. I signed a contract paying me about $15,000 a month, which worked out to well under $200,000 a year, a fraction of my NBA high of more than $3 million my last year in Sacramento.

The Russian league was very physical, more than the other leagues I played in overseas. But it was the same as other countries in that the team's focus was making the local players look good, even if that meant keeping much more highly skilled Americans on the bench or diminishing their roles.

We won the Russian Cup, the championship trophy that was a big deal there. As a matter of fact, that team still owes me more than $40,000, a bonus my contract said I was due if the team won the championship. (Since the team went bankrupt in 2008, I guess I'm never seeing that money.)

Over the next seven years, from 2004 to 2011, I played for four different clubs overseas: Sedima Roseto in Italy, Aris BC in Greece, Al-Ittihad in Saudi Arabia, and Kyoto Hannaryz in Japan. That $15,000 a month became my reality in every country. Once your price is set, it's hard to escape it. I always played well, averaging more than 20 points per game when I wasn't hurt and when I was getting game time.

In Greece, I saw how other players began to perceive my skills as lacking because I was stuck on the bench. It was humiliating spending so much time watching from the sidelines. One day in practice, the team's starting point guard — an American who'd had a stellar career overseas — said something to me with a dismissive tone, implying that I was washed up and I couldn't handle him. I was incensed. The coaches were watching us closely at the time. I chuckled to myself — what I sometimes do to calm myself down — but I felt compelled to respond because of how I felt the head coach, in particular, was treating me. This player was falling into the trap of thinking I was washed up because I wasn't playing much and because when I did play, they were trying to force me into playing like a robot in order to get minutes. These types of challenges can go either way, but I was determined to make it go mine.

"I tell you what," I said. "Let's go to five. Your ball first."

As he eyed me, I added, "This is gonna be an easy game."

I don't usually trash talk like that, but this guy had me so enraged that I felt it necessary to up the ante. We squared off and he proceeded to miss his first shot. That was the last time he touched the ball. *Bam, bam, bam, bam, bam.* The ball never even touched the rim. After I whupped him, I stared at him.

"Don't you ever in your life disrespect me again and assume that you could even come close to me," I said loudly, aware that the coaches were watching us. I pointed at the coaches and said, "They know it, too! Don't confuse the fact that because they're not playing me that I don't have it. You know better. And they know better."

I glared at the coaches as I said it because I wanted to send a message. I guess the message was received, but not in the way I wanted. The coach called me into his office and subtly threatened to let me go if I didn't play like he wanted—a robot who was just there to set up other players. I got a lot less time after that day. In one of the games, they even gave me some kind of award, in honor of my career. It was an expensive piece of sculpture. After the game, I never saw the sculpture again. I'm still waiting on it all these years later. I got the spot picked out on my mantel for it—if ever it shows up.

Playing in Saudi Arabia was a gratifying experience. The weather was nice, and the team practiced only once a day—a lot of the overseas clubs practiced twice a day, which I suspect was to keep tabs on the players as much as possible. Plus, I didn't have any difficulty finding foods that were halal, or "permissible" in accordance with the Quran.

However, the level of competition there was well below what I was used to—more like a top-notch high school team. The games were also odd because typically there were very few people in the stands. The gyms looked like the games that were played during COVID, with as few as five or six people in attendance at times, and no women were allowed. It felt like we were at practice or something. In Saudi Arabia, I was easily averaging well over 20 points, but it still was a system where they highlight their own guys.

For the first time in my life, I was living in a place where I didn't have to experience winter weather. But there were things about the society that felt wrong and odd to me, such as the way women were treated. They couldn't drive a car, yet they could perform surgery at a hospital. It didn't make any sense.

Things went bad for me in Saudi Arabia when, once again, I decided to speak my mind instead of going along with the program. It involved a troubling incident with a big man named Marvin Stone from Huntsville, Alabama, who had come over to play on the team. Apparently, Marvin had heart issues. (We found out later his father had died of a heart attack at age forty-seven and one of his sisters died during a heart operation at age thirty-two.) He and I lived in the same hotel, which contained units that were more like apartments: kitchen, living room, dining room, two bedrooms. I would pick him up and take him to practice. During halftime in one of the games, while the coach was talking, I noticed Marvin slithering down in his chair next to me and slobbering from his mouth. I thought he was having an epileptic seizure. People jumped up and started pouring water over his head.

"Quit pouring water over his head—he can't breathe!" I yelled.

He started shaking. I was trying to get everyone to back up and give Marvin space. "Call a doctor!" I said.

They're supposed to have doctors at these facilities, like in the NBA. But there were none on-site. We had about five guys carry him down the hall, and we stuffed him in an SUV to take him to the hospital. Marvin was 6'10", so he was bunched up in the SUV. I think he was dead before the SUV even left for the hospital.

The team concocted a story about what happened, but they weren't telling the whole truth. I think they were trying to protect themselves so they wouldn't have to pay the family money. I got pissed off. So when the Associated Press called me, just like with Bernard Goldberg, I said exactly what I was thinking. I told the reporter that they didn't have a doctor at the facility and there was no ambulance. I said we stuffed him in an SUV and that I thought he was dead before the vehicle took off. I told the reporter that the team needed to take care of his family.

Guess what? The Saudi team didn't ask me to come back the next year. I took another year off before I went to Kyoto, Japan. That was such a vastly different basketball scene from those in the other countries. The talent there was above Saudi Arabia but below the EuroLeague, and it was so stress-free. The people of Japan were incredibly welcoming. It was the first time in my life playing basketball where, no matter if we were winning or losing, no one ever booed, on the road or at home. And amazingly, your fans gave you gifts after the game. I had numerous families who would bring me things, like baskets of fruit, chocolate, cookies. They knew I loved mangoes, so they often brought me mangoes and strawberries. When I left the gym, I'd often have bags of presents. It was the best crowd I'd ever experienced.

Some guys assumed that because the fans didn't boo and brought you gifts, they were ignorant to your on-court performance. Guys got caught up thinking, *Oh, they love me here! They love us regardless of how we play!* And they'd soon find themselves on the chopping block or getting traded when they weren't performing. I understood that and never took the crowd for granted. I played two years in Kyoto, the only overseas club that invited me back even though I was forty-one by the time I finished my second season there in 2011. I was still in great shape, but I figured it was time to move on to the next chapter of my life.

CHAPTER 23

During my years overseas, I had several more kids, increasing my family to five children. It was what I had dreamed of when I was young: a houseful of squealing, amusing, rambunctious, loving kids. Ali was born in 1999, Alim in 2000, Ammar in 2001, Safiyyah (my only daughter) in 2003, and Amir in 2005.

Every time I had to leave the house to get back on an airplane, it was painful. I maintained a love-hate relationship with basketball. I loved the fact that I got the opportunity to go play and earn a living so I could feed them and keep a nice roof over their heads. But at the same time, it hurt me to leave them. I would have to put on my game face to be able to get through it, to keep moving without being pulled down by depression.

In March 2003, when I was thirty-four, I lost my mother right before Safiyyah was born. Mom never told us she was sick. I noticed that her belly was protruding; I figured maybe she was pregnant. Yes, she was in her fifties, but women in their fifties can get pregnant. She had a boyfriend at the time—I mean, things happen. With that bit of weirdness in the back of my mind, I was going about my business; she was going about hers. All of a sudden, one day she was admitted into the hospital. I rushed to the hospital, wondering what had suddenly made her so sick.

When I got there, I saw a bunch of my family members, including her sister Liz, as I walked into the room and looked around. "Hey, what's going on, guys?" I said, sounding upbeat.

Liz pulled me aside. "Mahmoud, can I talk to you?" she said. We went outside the hospital room to chat.

"I don't know if your mother told you," she said.

"Told me what?" I was so oblivious.

She looked me in the eyes. "Your mother has stage four cancer. Ovarian cancer," she said.

"Whaaat?!" My eyes immediately began to water. "What are you talking about?"

She nodded. "Yeah, she's been dealing with this for a while now."

I went back into the room in a daze. As politely as I could, I said, "If y'all don't mind, can I talk to my mother for a minute?"

I moved close to the bed when the room cleared out.

"Mom—" Just saying that one word made me start to cry. "Mom, why didn't you tell me?" I could barely get the words out of my mouth.

I told her about a doctor in Houston, one I had read about before I even heard her diagnosis, who had been successful in curing many different forms of cancer. The federal government wouldn't allow him to transport his practice outside of Texas.

"That's how damn corrupt and unjust the system is," I said. "Mom, let's go to Houston. Let me take you there."

She answered, sounding very weak. "No, baby. I'mma be okay."

"Mom, please." I could hardly get the words out, I was crying so hard.

Now she was trying to console me. "It's going to be all right, baby." I stayed with her for a few more minutes before everybody came back into the room. I was devastated. It had come at me so fast. We got a nurse to come to her house, so she could return home. But that didn't feel right to me.

"Mom, why don't you just come and stay with us?" I asked her.

Eventually she gave in. I knew it was hard for her. She just had a strong streak of independence stamped on her DNA. She had spent her adult life taking care of us as a single parent; she had a hard time letting go, allowing someone to take care of her. The day I brought her to our house, I was trying to keep her upbeat, thinking it would do her good to be around her grandchildren. But she got sicker and didn't even stay a full night.

Back in the hospital, I was with her constantly, sleeping on the little couch there in the room. Although she had this great strength, she also had a soft teddy-bear side that she didn't let many people see. She was getting so skinny and so weak, and it was hard for her to stand up—but she still had a hard time letting me help her. She would slap me on the arm and yell, "I got it!"

I would help her into the bathroom and turn around as she did her business. But every time, she would slap me and tell me to stop helping. Finally, I had had enough.

"Listen!" I said, raising my voice. "Dammit, I know you strong! And I know that you prefer to do this on your own. This isn't what you prefer. Mom, this ain't taking nothing away from your strength and who you are as a woman. This is just necessary, all right? Let me help you! Ain't nothing wrong with that."

When I said that, it kind of released her; from that moment she allowed me to help her. That very night, I was drifting off to sleep on the couch when I heard a commotion.

"We're losing her! We're losing her!" Those were the words I heard when I woke up. I saw my mother in the bed gasping for air, trying to hold on. I rushed over to her side.

"Mom, I love you," I said, looking into her face. "Let it go. It's okay to let go. I love you so much."

I kept repeating that I loved her. Within minutes, she was gone.

Once she passed, I went into the hallway and called my brother David. "David, we just lost her," I said.

I left the hospital and drove home in the dark of night, dealing with sadness and fatigue.

When I reached home, I got into bed with my wife, my head still in a daze. I thought about my childhood, all the years of struggle, and how my mom managed to keep things going. This woman who meant everything to me was now gone. I prayed silently, thinking about death, thinking about all the things we would have to do the next day.

We had her services at the grave site. I told them I didn't want her casket to be open, as my mother was a very private woman. People questioned me on that decision, but I held fast, certain it's what she would have desired. I wanted every detail to represent who she was. When I spoke at the funeral, I talked about how we are so quick to say that when people die, they are in a better place.

"I don't know that," I said. "I love my mother. I love her dearly. I don't know if she's in a better place. I can only pray that God has mercy on her soul and that he forgives her like I ask God to forgive me and have mercy on my soul."

My brother David and a cousin of ours also spoke. We then lowered her body into the grave. Then we all went back to my house and ate. Talked. My brother and I had to start thinking about what we were going to do with her house and all her stuff. That was tough, man. It all was very tough.

In 2005, my wife and I decided we wanted to leave Mississippi and move to Atlanta. We sold our house in Pass Christian and moved into an apartment in Gulfport while we drove back and forth to Atlanta, trying to figure out where we wanted to buy. We hadn't been in the apartment for more than a month when we started getting warnings in late August that a severe hurricane was headed for the Gulf. We decided to drive to Nashville to wait out the storm. Hurricane Katrina roared through the Gulf Coast and made history with its ferocity and destruction. The National Hurricane Center estimated the total number of deaths to be 1,833, though the number is still debated because hundreds more people disappeared and were never accounted for. In Mississippi, at least 238 people died, including 126 deaths in Harrison County, the coastal county that includes Gulfport and Biloxi. It continues to be the costliest and one of the five deadliest hurricanes to ever strike the United States.

When we returned to Gulfport to assess the damage, we saw apartment units that had been totally wiped out. In our apartment, which was a little farther from the shore, the water was above waist-deep; in my mother-in-law's apartment nearby, the water had gotten up to the ceiling. There were apartments with markings on the door; we were told they indicated that people had died there.

In Atlanta, we stayed with April's sister, Vicky, and her husband, Shawn, for a couple of months before we bought a place. My son Amir, my youngest child, was born in December of that year.

When we moved to Atlanta, I should have bought the house we moved into outright in cash, but I went against my better judgment and financed it. I had other properties in Mississippi I had bought outright, and the return on the money was up and down because of inconsistency with renters. The money I had stashed away started dwindling, which was even more incentive for me to go overseas. I went to play in Greece in 2006, when I was thirty-seven years old, but when I got back things were still tight. I was seriously embarrassed, humiliated, but despite a pain that almost felt like an ulcer, I gritted my teeth and called a few of my NBA guys. Hakeem Olajuwon sent me $25,000. Shareef Abdur-Rahim sent me $100,000. I now had some breathing room while I figured out a plan.

Things were okay for the next few years. We had money in

the bank. But one day I was training at LA Fitness in Atlanta, after I had finished my two years in Japan, and I got a call from my wife. She almost sounded like she was hyperventilating.

"We're in the red," she said.

"What? What do you mean, 'We're in the red'?" Of course I knew what that phrase meant, but I was hoping she was playing, even though I sensed she wasn't, or maybe she'd used the wrong word.

"We don't have any money," she said. "Nothing."

"What do you mean, nothing? We had thousands in the bank. I just got through playing. Where did it go?!"

A few years earlier I had given her access to the money for the first time. Before that, it was like you have yours, I have mine, and we have a joint account. But we had been married for well over a decade and she wanted more responsibility, so I gave it to her. What she was now telling me was almost unbelievable. I was devastated. I kept asking her where the money went, but she couldn't give me an answer. I found that strange and suspicious. If it went to pay bills, there should be a paper trail of bills paid. We were going through a rocky period in our marriage. My mind began to grab for explanations. Maybe she'd stashed away money in case things didn't work out between us. Or maybe she'd given a major loan to her mother or one of her family members and didn't want to tell me. But her saying "I don't know" was unacceptable. On that day, I was so close to asking her for a divorce.

"What are we going to do? We, you, have to do something," she said.

I responded, "I can't just make money appear with the snap of my fingers. It doesn't work like that."

I was beyond embarrassed that I was now in this position— yet another Black athlete who had squandered millions. I was at a loss for what to do. I had the house note coming in and no means to pay it.

My body was racked with so much tension and worry, a smothering heaviness that is difficult to describe. I was concerned that I would get another ulcer. Despite my shame, I started making phone calls.

I sat on the garage steps and called Salahuddeen Abdul Kareem, who had moved to Gaithersburg, Maryland, and who had been like a father to me throughout most of my years playing professional basketball. I asked him to keep us in his *dua* prayers because I had just received news from my wife that we were literally dead broke.

"Right now, outside of praying to Allah, I don't know what to do," I said. I told him I was calling to vent and ask that favor of him to make a *dua*, but I should have known he was going to get on the phone and make calls. Within maybe a few days or a week — it seemed like a long time — I received a couple of important calls. One of them was from an imam who has communities in Southeast D.C. and Oakland. He told me that over the years when I would come and help them with fundraisers and donate money, they had put some of the money away for a rainy day. Now the rains had come. He sent me over $30,000. Another close friend, a very private brother, flew down to Atlanta and handed me $30,000 in cash. I was so grateful.

When I was at LA Fitness working out one afternoon, some-body asked me to train his son. I trained myself constantly, but outside of giving tips, I hadn't officially considered training some-body else. I had no idea how much to charge, and I had to figure out how to train someone without killing them. This is when my training career commenced. News of my unusual but very effective regimen began to spread by word of mouth; the requests started pouring in. A company called me to work with NBA player Ben Gordon. That led me to other NBA players who wanted me to train them. In addition, I was getting a ton of requests to train college and high school players.

Around the same time, I got a call from someone who wanted

me to give a speech to his organization in Paterson, New Jersey. I had no idea what to charge for that, either, but I came up with an amount that felt right at the time. Then I got another speaking request— this time somebody filmed it and put the video online. After that, I started getting so many requests that I decided to work with a booking agent. I knew I couldn't let the public know of my money woes because people would start asking for my services on the cheap. That's how capitalism works.

I spent a lot of time praying to God: *Please bring me out of this. Please don't expose my flaws in this condition to the world. Bless me to learn from this. Give me patience. Give me understanding. Let me persevere. Bless me to come out of this. Please, God.*

People would see me at the gym and have no idea what I was going through. I always had a ready smile for people that didn't reveal my stress. One day I was walking out of the gym to my car. I had already given up my Infiniti SUV. I had enough money from time to time to rent a car. On this day, I was in a run-of-the-mill rental, living as simply as possible. A guy was walking next to me, and when we got to the car, he looked at me confused, and asked, "Is this your car?"

With a smile, I said, "Yes, my bro."

"That's what I love about you!" he said very excitedly.

"What are you talking about?" I asked.

"All that money you made, and nobody would even know because you keep it simple," he said.

Now my appearance wasn't totally a fabrication because years ago before retiring I decided to simplify my life. But the way I was living when he saw me was well below the standard I had planned for myself.

I smiled back, but inside I felt the embarrassment of knowing that my public perception was much different from what was going on in private. I was waiting to turn forty-five in 2014 so I could access my NBA pension. The struggle went on for the next few years — me making just enough to pay the bills and keep a roof over my family's heads. My kids and I often had to jump the gate at the local activity center in the neighborhood to shower before school. This was incredibly humiliating for me, and I know it was for my children, too.

As if that wasn't bad enough, one day while I was in Dallas at a speaking engagement for a Malcolm X program, I got a phone call from my wife. "We're moving out," she said. "Why are you doing that?" I asked. "Listen, that don't make sense. If anything, let me move out. You can stay in the house with the children."

But when I got back home, they were all gone. I was in that big house by myself, struggling to pay the bills. I started getting foreclosure notices, once again reminding me that I should have bought the house outright when I had the money. I found myself subsisting on a diet that included a lot of rice and beans. Suddenly, I was back to my Mississippi childhood. That thought was even more mortifying for me.

They cut off my gas, so I couldn't even turn on the heat when the days grew colder. I gathered all the candles I could find and set them up around the living room while I shivered on the couch, buried under comforters. After a couple weeks of freezing cold nights, it dawned on me that the candles would work a lot better if I stayed in a smaller room. I gathered them up and went into the bathroom. I was a lot warmer in there, sleeping on the floor surrounded by the flickering candles. Of course, when I stepped out of the bathroom, the rest of the house was frigid.

Since I didn't have a car, I would sometimes rely on people to give me rides to the gym. But my pride prevented me from doing that too often. If somebody at the gym offered to drive me home, I usually would refuse, telling them the walking was part of my training routine. But the real reason was I just didn't want people to know. I didn't want anyone to feel sorry for me. My thinking was that I had put myself in this situation; it was my job to get myself out of it. I was trying real hard to fathom the lesson this was supposed to be teaching me. I know Allah tests us in many ways—what was I supposed to be learning from my deprivation?

After a while, as the speaking engagements got more lucrative and the training requests poured in, I was able to crawl out of the hole. I was able to eat, to survive. Then I turned forty-five and got my NBA pension. The penalty was steep for not waiting until I was fifty-five. It should have been more than $600,000, but with the penalty I got a little over $300,000.

Soon after, things got tough for me again: April and I decided to divorce. In actuality, the slow implosion of our marriage had begun many years earlier, before I went to play in Turkey in 1998. Just before I was to leave, we were sitting in a restaurant on the beach in Gulfport and April said, "Listen, I want to say something."

"Okay, what is it?"

"Listen, just let me finish," she said. "I'm putting my big-girl drawers on."

"Okay, what do you want to tell me?" I asked, half giggling.

"I know how you are. I know you have a high sex drive." She paused. "If you're out in Turkey and you see someone that you want to be with, just don't let me know about it."

Whoa. That was not at all what I expected to hear coming out of her mouth, two years into our marriage.

"I appreciate that, but that wasn't my intention," I said.

Two years in, I was committed to trying to remain monogamous. I had been focused on working out, playing ball, being disciplined. But when she opened that door, psychologically it changed my whole mindset. In Islam, a man may have more than one wife, up to four wives simultaneously, but there are so many spiritual, mental, emotional, financial, and physical dynamics to consider for it to be legitimate. However, I wasn't planning on going into that room of possibilities—but when she opened that door, I became more curious to see what was inside. I did get involved in a relationship with a woman in Turkey. April found out about it. She was visibly upset for three or four days, but then she was back to her normal self. It is important to note that all of these relationships while I was married were Islamic relationships.

Nine years later in 2007, right before I was to leave to play in Saudi Arabia, April made the same offer, except this time she said she wanted to know about it if I went down that road. Later, April asked me whether I had met anyone I would want to spend time with. I told her that I had. She was twenty-five years old, a Somali nurse. I'll call her Anissa. After that conversation, I began to pursue a relationship with Anissa, and it became serious. So serious that she asked if she could be my second wife. But I told her even though my wife knew about her, April was not ready for that step—God knows I wish she was. April called one night when I was with Anissa—we were returning from eating out—and asked if she was with me now. I said yes; she calmly asked me to call back when I was finished. That's when I knew at least on the surface that she was processing this much differently from before.

Before finishing my last year in Japan in 2011, I started to feel like the bonds of the marriage were beginning to fray. I think the phrase "absence makes the heart grow fonder" was applicable in my case for so many years. Being away so much, I believe, helped my marriage last a lot longer than it would have if I were home all the time. I began to notice there was a serious intellectual gap between us that started to create an emotional and physical rift that got worse and worse.

One day I expressed to April what I noticed and how it made

me feel. I told her, "Listen, you know Allah tells us to lower our gaze and guard our modesty. But I'm having issues right now. I'm starting to see myself looking at women more, and I don't want to do that. I'm not gawking. I don't let them know I'm looking. But I don't like the way this feels because I shouldn't be doing it.

"I'm coming to you; I'm opening up to you," I continued. "In my own way, I'm crying out that I need you."

"Mahmoud, we've been married almost sixteen years," she said. "You wanted it a lot when we were first married, and you would think that would wind down. But damn, you done picked it up." She shook her head. "You ain't normal."

I told her I could understand how she might feel that way. But it was more than just sexual. "Yes, I need you to pick it up sexually. But I also need you to engage me more intellectually. Before we got married, we had this conversation, and I said our first objective should be getting closer to God, closer to Allah, because if we do that, then I believe everything else will fall into place. Once you lose the intellectual connection, eventually what's going to happen is there's going to be a physical gap. It's natural.

"You don't have to like things the same way as me, but if we say this is our faith, sometimes I'm wanting to talk to you about stuff like what Allah says, what's going on in the world," I said. "I get it—this ain't what you do. You don't read like that. But I feel like you're patronizing me; you're not really engaging me. Because you're giving me the same answer for about fifteen, sixteen years. You go, 'Oh, okay, that's nice. *Mashallah. Alhamdulillah.*' But you ain't giving me nothing. I want to learn, too. I want to be inspired; I want to be challenged. You know what I mean? I just don't want to be the one giving. I want to hear your thoughts. I'm calling my guys to get that, but I want it from you. I want us to have it. I want to give it to our children. Right now, I'm not getting that."

I told her sometimes I would turn over in bed to tell her about something exciting I had just read, but then I'd think about whom I'm talking to and just turn back around.

"If you can, I need you to help me with that. Because right now, my mind is starting to look at other scenarios, other women."

As I predicted, eventually I got involved with a beautiful young lady I met at the gym. When April found out, she had a hard time with it. It was much different from the other relationships because it was so close to home. She even pressed me to let her meet the young lady. I knew that was a bad idea, but I relented. When she came home after meeting her at Starbucks, she said the woman was indeed gorgeous and she could understand why I was attracted to her. But it was clear our marriage was approaching the finish line. April started to lose weight; she was very troubled by it all. One day when we were in the kitchen, things got heated between us.

"Look, let's just forget it, man. We need a divorce," I said.

She looked at me closely. "Oh, really?"

"Yeah," I said.

But then I thought about it and came back to her ten minutes later. "You know what? I think it's something we could work out," I said.

"No, no, we need a divorce," she said.

"Now you're being reactionary."

"No, you asked for it. You wanted it," she said.

Several months later, we agreed to part ways. The marriage was over. I sold a property in Mississippi and gave her half of the proceeds. Then I gave her a bunch of the money from the NBA pension to close out our divorce settlement. I stayed in an InTown Suites for a year because I didn't want to rush into buying another house.

My public speaking gigs really began to take off at this point. The invitations initially came mostly from the Muslim community, like Islamic schools and organizations. They wanted me to speak about my life, how I came to Islam. I would start out talking about my childhood and my struggles and my questioning Christianity. I would say that even before I became a Muslim, even before I knew what the *fajr* prayer (the dawn prayer) was, I would wake up before dawn to go train—in effect preparing myself for my future reversion. When I was a young person going through these struggles, I truly believe they were preparing me for something much bigger and more important: my reversion to Islam.

I was invited to speak at a school in New Jersey, then later that evening a brother named Wali brought me to a masjid in New York to give another speech. I didn't even realize Wali was filming me at the masjid. After he posted a video of the speech on YouTube, where it got a ton of hits, my phone really started ringing. The requests were now also coming from groups that weren't connected to the Muslim community—humanitarian organizations asking me to speak in Palestine, in Africa. I was getting requests from elite universities like Rutgers, Harvard, and Yale and from colleges up in the cut that I had never heard of. I was so busy, I was going out almost every week. I would often come home with more than I gave, because after a speech I would talk to people and they would share information with me. I would ask people to recommend books for me to read; I was constantly in bookstores, gathering more books, more information. I would read books on a wide variety of topics— politics, history, health—that I possibly never would have come across on my own.

Things picked up even more when President Donald Trump started going after Colin Kaepernick. When issues like controversy over the national anthem hit the news, there's a tendency for people to want to look back, to reach into the nation's history to see if there were any precedents for this, any people who did similar things in the past. Guys like me and Tommie Smith and John Carlos, who became cultural icons after their raised-fist protest at the Mexico City Olympics in 1968, become hotter commodities. With all the racial protests and reckoning, my speaking requests continued at a steady pace. I was making a very good living giving speeches before the Kaepernick controversy, but afterward it grew exponentially. Even though we all need to make a living, I was hyperconscious never to make it about the money; it had to be about the issues.

Eventually I found a house in Georgia that fit my needs. It was a little farther away from Atlanta than I wanted — about forty minutes from the city — but it had six bedrooms, three baths, and sat on an acre lot. It was too good to pass up. Plenty of room for me and all the kids. By now I had enough money stashed to buy the house outright. No mortgage — just the way I like it. Things started getting even better for me financially: I was getting money from a variety of sources, including the NBA 2K video game and the NBA.

I was in a much better space, but I'll never forget that feeling of humiliation from being broke and trying to keep it a secret. There's a belief that Allah tests more those whom he loves the most. I don't know if that's the case with me, because the evil ones are tested, too. But I do believe Allah knows my intention; he knows I mean well and I want to commit myself to him, to be righteous and do what's right. I want to stand up for justice. Any time you struggle, I think it brings you closer to God. So maybe with the way I was living, my choices, Allah was shaking me, telling me that I had to be more mindful, more diligent, more responsible, more disciplined.

The pain and humiliation all reminded me of how serious my relationship is with Allah. For that, I am grateful.

CHAPTER 24

A few years back, I was at the gym working out when a friend of mine mentioned that a new three-on-three league was being started. He thought I should look into it, but I wasn't interested. I thought it would be another attempt at a basketball league that wouldn't go anywhere. When I started hearing more about this Big3 league, I saw that it was becoming closer to a reality. Then Ice Cube announced in January 2017 that the league would debut that year. This league of former players became official. My friend Chauncey Ashford, whom we call C.J., came to me as an unofficial emissary for the league.

"Man, they really want you to come try out," he said. "No politics."

"Don't tell me that, because mostly everything is political — if not everything," I said. "And a lot of times when people say it's not political, it's probably going to be more politics."

But I relented. "Okay, I'll go. No problem."

He sent me the paperwork and I signed their waiver. I met him in Las Vegas for the tryouts. I was forty-eight at the time, one of the oldest players in the gym, but I was in great shape. I had several people come up to me and exclaim about the shape I was in. They had us play three-on-three during the tryouts. I don't think I missed a shot. But when they started making the selections, I saw it was going to be exactly what I feared: guys who were seriously out of shape and shouldn't have even been there were getting picked up by their buddies. I was sitting there watching one player after another go up, and my name still hadn't been called. *Are you serious, man?* I thought.

The 3 Headed Monster squad was down to their last pick. My friend C.J. was sitting with them. He told me they were about to pick a dude who was basically the same player as Rashard Lewis, the 6'10" former All-Star who was looking to be one of their top players.

"Why are you going to pick him?" C.J. said. "He's the same player as you, Rashard. Y'all only got one guard, man. What if your guard goes down?"

They turned to C.J. "You're right. Who should we pick?"

"Mahmoud, man! He been killin' the whole camp!"

Their pick was about to be announced. They interrupted the guy to say they were changing the pick. C.J. said they were like, "Wait! Wait!" I didn't see any of that going on before I finally heard my name called. If C.J. hadn't been there, I wouldn't have even played in the Big3.

Stephen Jackson, the former NBA player who was selected by the Killer 3s (who is now Muslim), joked to me, "Man, y'all ain't even gonna win a game!"

Well, we went to the finals that first season, going 6–2 before losing that last game. Initially, our coach, the Hall of Famer Gary Payton, wasn't playing me much. Then Jason Williams, the flashy white guard who went by the nickname "White Chocolate," suffered an injury and couldn't play. Jason was more of an open-court player, not particularly adept in half-court, which was a space where I thrived. I don't think Jason was into it that much anyway. But his injury forced Gary to put me in. By the grace and mercy of Allah, my shot was falling; it was hard for him to not play me. On the stat sheet, I finished second in the league in assists, second in steals, and seventh in total field goals (Rashard led the league in total points and field goals).

Eventually I got upgraded to cocaptain, which meant that my spot in subsequent years was guaranteed and I wouldn't have to try out again (something I said I was not going to do). Gary was an incredible player, but he is a hard-nosed guy and we didn't exactly mesh. However, the league has been a positive experience for me — playing for the Big3 has introduced me to a younger crowd who wouldn't have known anything about me. The league pays $10,000 a weekend, which basically means $10,000 per game; flies you in first class; puts you up in top-notch hotels; and gives you per diem cash. You have the potential to make $100,000 for the season if you get to the championship game.

In 2017, when I was being honored at the National Association of Black Journalists convention in New Orleans, my old LSU coach, Dale Brown, got up to speak. Coach was the only white person in the audience. He went up on the stage and told the crowd that the only reason my jersey hadn't been retired at LSU was because I'm Muslim. For him to say that, a white guy who has spent years in those white circles of money and influence, it means that he's surely heard things.

Coach Brown had mentioned to me in the past that my LSU jersey needed to be retired. Shaquille had an actual statue at the school, but I think Shaq gave the university $2 million. I wasn't about to give it $2 million. If anything, the school made so much money off us, it owed us money. I never pushed for the jersey retirement or spent much time dwelling on it. When people asked me about it, I would say that a part of me didn't care. I can't take that accolade to God at the pearly gate and say, "I averaged 30.2 points as a freshman and I got my jersey retired at LSU." That's not going to help me on the Day of Judgment. But on the other hand, I did want it to happen, because if it didn't, it would be part of the tradition of erasing and denying our history. If my jersey was up there, some kid may come along and see my name in the rafters and ask, "Who is he? Let me go do some research about him."

I had mixed emotions about it, but somebody who didn't was an LSU alumna named Katrina Dunn, a Black doctor in California who was the main catalyst behind the drive to get my jersey retired.

She told me, "Mahmoud, this has to be done. Do I have your permission to push for this? What do you think?"

I told her that part of me didn't care, but part of me did. "If this is something you feel you want to push, I'll support you a hundred percent," I said.

I wasn't going to beg. That's just not in my DNA.

She said that they needed to bring me back to campus to give a speech, so I did an event with the Black Students Association, giving the Black History Month keynote. There were several high-ranking LSU officials in the audience. During the question-and-answer period, I was asked how LSU could do a better job of connecting with former LSU athletes.

I answered that the school should be reaching out more to former players. Then I recounted a conversation I had with a guy who had played basketball for Kentucky. We had played against each other in high school.

"He said they have a program at Kentucky that even if you've been out of school for twenty years, the alumni put money into a fund that allows you to come back and get your degree if you want."

I said. "It's paid for in full. They find you a job if you need a job. Something that fits what you can do. I said that's a university that hasn't forgotten. They care about more than what you did on the basketball court."

I said that if my son came to me and told me he was deciding between LSU and Kentucky, I'd send him to Kentucky.

"Because it's always bigger than the game," I said. "And everybody wants to feel they're needed."

Once the decision was actually made to retire my jersey, I wasn't surprised, because it was making them look bad that they hadn't done it. People would walk into the arena and see the jerseys of Shaq, Rudy Macklin, Pistol Pete, and Bob Pettit and wonder, *Where's Mahmoud*? If I'm a parent and you're recruiting my son and I know anything about Chris Jackson/Mahmoud Abdul-Rauf—and you've just given me the "we care about our players; this is a family" speech—when I look up, I'm going to think it's odd that the name Jackson or Abdul-Rauf isn't there. This player who set an NCAA record that's been unbroken for more than thirty years. Where is he? What can LSU say in answer to that? So, no, I don't think the decision was out of some sense of altruism, love, or appreciation. They were pressured. But that's okay; do it anyway.

I got a call from the school, asking me what name I wanted on the back of the number 35 jersey.

"I want the name I am now: Mahmoud Abdul-Rauf," I said.

The name was a choice I made. We didn't have a choice with the name Jackson; it was a relic of slavery. I was taking ownership of who I am and what it means: "elegant," "praise-worthy," "servant of the most kind."

At the ceremony, Pettit and Macklin were there, in addition to Maravich's wife. Shaquille spoke in a prerecorded video that was shown on the big screen, during which he called me "the greatest player to ever play at LSU."

"I learned a lot from you," he said. "I appreciate you playing with me. I appreciate you showing me how to be great. This is your moment, brother. Love you and talk to you soon. As-salaamu alaykum."

During my speech, I said I could never have written this story for myself, to be in this position thirty years later. I thanked a bunch of people for making it happen, including Coach Brown for "talking the issue up" over many years. However, I forgot to mention Katrina Dunn in my speech; I was so upset with myself and would later apologize to her.

"But most importantly I wouldn't be here without my mother, who was my nurturer, who was my first educator, who was my protector, who was my provider," I said. "And I'm always trying to be careful when I mention her name because ninety percent of the time I can't help but start crying when I do so, 'cause she meant that much to me.

"Growing up, there's always things that motivate you," I said a bit later in the speech, when I got teary-eyed. "Trying to make it to the top, you want to feed your family, you want to help people. But [my children] were my inspiration. Growing up without a father, I would wake up and I would train, relentlessly. Because one of my goals was to have a family someday. And to be able to raise children."

At this point, while I was surrounded by four of my kids, the tears started flowing — so much that Safiyyah started wiping them from my face as I talked. "So I just wanted them to know, even though they weren't there through all of those years of training, they were always in the back of my mind. And I wanted them to experience this moment."

If I'm giving a speech about my mom or my children, I always have to fight back the tears. My family was such a huge part of my pushing myself out of bed in the morning during my childhood training sessions. When I think back on the progression of my life, the fact that I did it all so that I could one day raise a family of my own means that, in the end, I realized my greatest dream. Yes, I wanted to be wealthy, I wanted to have things, I wanted to help people, to give to the poor. But most of all, I wanted to have a family of my own to cherish.

My life has been a powerful lesson in the grace that comes from faith, from giving back, from struggle, perseverance, patience, living, and dying with a free conscience and a free soul. I know there may be many people who don't understand or agree with the positions I take or the things I say, but no one will ever be able to say I didn't speak my conscience and that I didn't stand for something. I'm not perfect—none of us are. I don't always make the best decision—none of us do. My goal has always been to teach and to learn. To stay learning, every single day of my life.

ACKNOWLEDGMENTS

There are so many people who played an important role—big or small—in shaping my life. I'm certain that due to the passage of time, some names will undoubtedly and unintentionally not be mentioned, only to be remembered later and visited with remorse. I apologize in advance. Your contributions God knows best, and He is the best of record keepers. With that said, I'd like to acknowledge the following people:

My ex-wife, April Dotson, who blessed me with my children. My grandmother Myrtle Jackson and grandfather Stephen Jackson, who began the process of bringing us with God's help into existence. Aunt Delores Cleveland, Elizabeth Cleveland, Vivian Cleveland, Rodgers Cleveland, Patrick Cleveland, Aunt "Steem," cousin Robin Jackson, always hyping me up to believe big, and cousin Qwen Jackson. Aunt Carrie, Aunt Mary Knight and "Uncle" Sammy, Aunt Tony, Aunt Sonya and "Uncle" Anthony and their children, Aunt Antone and "Uncle" Larry Lewis and their children. Uncle Robert and Dorothy and their children, Uncle Russell, Uncle Fredrick, Mrs. Osaletta "Cookie," "Pop," Uncle Len for defending, protecting, and taking me to LSU against the will of many. Shaheed Ali "Shan," "Boo" Cooper, Mitchell Quince, Percy McClendon, Spencer, Dan Magee, Benny Magee, The Price family, Francisco "Boo" Hardy, Ms. Felicia "We We" Horn, Mr. and Mrs. Evans, Mrs. January and her family for being a solid support and mentor for me throughout my younger years. Dr. Dunn, Coach "Prince" Jones, for being tough on me and allowing me to consistently come in the gym and develop my skills with grown men, Coach Brazil, Mrs. Lindsay, Mr. Eddie Miller and Mrs. Miller and son Owen Miller, Mr. Magee, Mr. Lowenbauch, Ronnie Harris,

Ralph Coleman, Dionne Fortenberry, Leonard "Prunie" Bennett, Cliff Walker for his tireless support, Vic, Van and Angie Juzang, Feliz Lee, James Allen, James "Pookie" Tyler and Maurice Tyler, Coach Jenkins and Mrs. Jenkins, Coach Austin, Tony Norwood, Willie Locke, Mike Bogan, Ms. Olivers, Kelcie Banks, Morning Star Baptist Church, Dr. McNaire, David Lancaster, Coach Craig Carse, Coach Dale Brown, Coach Johnny Jones, Coach Ron Abernathy, Van and Rasul "Thyrone" Gross, Reggie Robinson, Mark Williams, "Tank" Lewis, Salahuddeen Abdul Kareem—a father I never had—and his wife Sister Hanifah and their children, Kim House, Muhammad Al Asi—a major mentor—Imam Musa, Bashir "Salam Books" Muhammad Shareef, Shareef Nasir, Hashim Alauddeen, Wali, Christy Casey, Patrice Spann, April Abdul-Rauf, the mother of all my children, Ricky Blanton, Vernel Singleton, Stanley Roberts, Shaquille O'Neal, Wayne Sims, Maurice Williamson, all my LSU teammates, Kaepernick Publishing, Howard Bryant, Sarah Allen, Nick Chiles, and Christopher Petrella.